John Joseph Valentine

Money

Natural law of money. International Bimetallism. Free Silver. Currency.

John Joseph Valentine

Money

Natural law of money. International Bimetallism. Free Silver. Currency.

ISBN/EAN: 9783744739566

Printed in Europe, USA, Canada, Australia, Japan

Cover: Foto ©Suzi / pixelio.de

More available books at **www.hansebooks.com**

MONEY.

NATURAL LAW OF MONEY.
INTERNATIONAL BIMETALLISM.
"FREE SILVER."
CURRENCY.

THE SILVER QUESTION AND HARD TIMES.

JOHN J. VALENTINE.

———————

"The coins which, being melted down,
retain the entire value for which they
were legal tender before being melted down,
are good money. Those which do not retain
it are not good money.

A coin is just as bad
when debased by overvaluation,
if not exchangeable for better,
as when unduly alloyed, clipped or sweated.

THIRD EDITION.

MONEY.

Natural Law of Money.
International Bimetallism.
"Free Silver."
Currency.

THE SILVER QUESTION

— AND —

HARD TIMES.

BY
JOHN J. VALENTINE.
5

INDEX.

PRESS OF
H. S. CROCKER COMPANY
SAN FRANCISCO

PREFACE.

THE four leading papers herein were incited by an admirable essay on the Bond Syndicate of 1895, read before the Berkeley Club of Oakland, at one of their stated meetings last winter, by Mr. Nye, of the Oakland *Enquirer*. The members of the Club, to whom I respectfully dedicate this little series of discourses, were so courteous as to voluntarily accord me an unusual allowance of time to speak upon the same subject; and, my remarks having led to a number of questions upon that and kindred matters, I at once decided to forego the preparation of a paper on Franz Deak, the Hungarian statesman, which I had in contemplation to serve at my turn to read before the Club, and substitute one upon the subject of money. My studies on this theme expanded into four separate papers, namely, The Natural Law of Money, International Bimetallism, Free Silver, and Currency, and they were listened to with such interest that I have been asked to publish them,—the honored President of the University of California, Prof. Martin Kellogg, having himself suggested that it was my duty to do so.

In yielding to these requests I would have it fully understood that I offer nothing novel or theoretical, for there is nothing new under the sun in regard to money, any more than there is in regard to other things, and here, as elsewhere, we have the lessons of experience to draw upon. I have, therefore, utilized in my remarks the expressions of well-known writers,

past and present,—John Locke, Adam Smith, Lord
Liverpool, Alexander Hamilton, Thomas Jefferson,
Albert Gallatin, Daniel Webster, Wm. Jacob, Jno. Stuart
Mill, Walter Bagehot, Henry D. MacLeod, Robert Giffen,
Prof. W. A. Shaw, Prof. Alfred Marshall, Benjamin
Kidd, Prof. Nicholson, Elijah Helm, William Brough,
Prof. McMaster, Prof. Shaler, Mr. Schoenhof, Horace
White, Andrew D. White of Cornell, Prof. Francis A.
Walker, Prof. Taussig, Prof. Farnham, Prof. Perry,
Prof. Hadley, Prof. Laughlin, Prof. Moses, David A.
Wells, C. F. Adams, Edward Atkinson, J. L. Greene,
R. Q. Mills, O. H. P. Belmont, Turnbull White, and
others too numerous to mention, not omitting, however,
my personal friend Louis A. Garnett, of this city, whom
I deem as well informed a man upon the subject as I
have ever come in contact with. I may add that, of the
French economists, Baisse, Levasseur, Chevalier, Parieu,
Permez, D'Avenal, the two Says, Leon and J. B., Tirard,
Beaulieu, des Essars, and more, there is not a single one
that was not, or is not, a supporter of the gold standard.

It is not for the purpose of making a pretence to
learning that I mention this formidable array of names,
but in order to give credit to these writers from whom,
as a constantly occupied business man, I have drawn,
often bodily. I think I may claim that few men have
been more steadily engaged than I during my forty-
two years of business activity, but having always
indulged a taste for reading, and been accustomed to
mark and note any item of statistical importance, or
argument which I particularly concurred in or dissented
from, it was not difficult for me to collect the facts cited
herein and draw my own conclusions from them.

The subject in all its bearings is one to which I have given some attention for more than thirty years, considerable of it since the discussion began in the seventies which ended in the passage of the Bland-Allison Act,—and which, in intervals of leisure since the passage of the so-called Sherman Act of July 14th, 1890, I have investigated with persistent, studious care. I came to its consideration with every possible motive for advocating the so-called cause of silver, but whatever may be thought of the influence of money on prices, or the feasibility of international bimetallism, however debatable that theory may be, or other monetary projects, it is an assured fact that the records of history and of economic science absolutely preclude the possibility of the concurrent circulation of gold and silver as legal tender under the independent, unlimited free coinage of both metals at a ratio of sixteen parts of silver to one part of gold, or at any ratio appreciably different from the commercial value of the metals,—and that under unlimited free coinage of silver by the United States alone the purchasing power of each coin would be confined to its bullion value, whatever that might be, from time to time.

A LAYMAN.

San Francisco, Cal.,
August 18, 1896.

PREFACE TO SECOND EDITION.

The first edition of this little book having been exhausted, a second is asked for, and in presenting it to an enlarged circle of readers it seems proper, in deference to such able and rational writers as Prof. J. S. Nicholson of Edinburgh, Mr. Elijah Helm of Manchester, and Prof. Francis A. Walker of Boston, to explain that the bimetallism, joint metallism or symmetallism advocated by them, or by Prof. Alfred Marshall, or such eminent Englishmen as, for example, Sir Samuel Montagu, are wholly different propositions from that now advanced by the Populistic free silver propagandists in the United States of America. See page 215.

On page 88 of the first edition, in first line on standard of value, the word "quality" was erroneously printed for *quantity*.

JOHN J. VALENTINE.

SAN FRANCISCO, CAL.,
September 5, 1896.

PREFACE TO THIRD EDITION.

The second edition of Money having been exhausted, and a third being called for, I have improved a little time and opportunity during the intervening month to include some additional touches that had been omitted before simply through the stress of other duties, official and private, and also to add the concluding two papers, which furnish their own explanation.

JOHN J. VALENTINE.

SAN FRANCISCO, CAL.,
October 3, 1896.

THE NATURAL LAW OF MONEY.

THE late Walter Bagehot remarked that the United States was a country for exemplifying by experiments on a large scale the old truths of political economy. The people were indifferent to experience gained elsewhere, while they were protected by their magnificent resources from the most serious consequences of mistakes in their own practices that in old countries would be supremely disastrous. They were thus constantly renewing old experiments under favorable conditions, and confirming, if *not* enlarging, the knowledge of the principles of political economy. The latest experiment of this kind is the silver legislation of which we have all heard so much.

It is not my design or expectation to present anything new or original in the consideration of this question, but simply some of the laws and established facts that govern it; and, in doing this, I have frequently utilized, without giving credit, the exact phraseology of the best writers upon the subject.

Of all things in the world, money, which can least bear tampering with or anything but scientific treatment, is being made in this country the bone of noisy contention, instigated partly by the influence of mining interests which ardently desire to raise the price of silver, and the adherents of a soft-money heresy who hope to create abundant money out of metal of some kind if they cannot have inconvertible paper.

The natural law of money is, in general, the law of civilization, viz, evolution: beginning, it may be, with the barter of a horse for a cow, a sheep for a hog, a goat for a dog; after that, the use of pebbles or shells as the representatives of value in the exchange of different commodities; next iron; then copper, bronze or brass; then silver; and finally gold, and obligations expressed on paper,—showing throughout a law of displacement, the inferior by the superior, or the survival of the fittest—gold—as the standard money—money of ultimate redemption, that metal having demonstrated to the world of commerce its superior utility, efficiency and refinement as the best basis and medium for the interchange of commodities, as well as for discharging the terms of time obligations.

Aristotle, on the origin and definition of money, says:

"It is plain that in the first society (that is, in the household) there was no such thing as barter, but that it took place when the community became enlarged; for the former had all things in common, while the latter, being separated, must exchange with each other according to their needs, just as many barbarous tribes now subsist by barter, for these merely exchange one useful thing for another, as, for example, giving and receiving wine for grain, and other things in like manner. From this it came about logically that as the machinery for bringing in what was wanted, and of sending out a surplus, was inconvenient, the use of money was devised as a matter of necessity. For not all the necessaries of life are easy of carriage; wherefore, to effect their exchanges, men contrived something to give and take among themselves *that which, being valuable in itself,* had the advantage of being easily passed from hand to hand for the needs of life, such as iron or silver, or something else of that kind, of which they first determined merely the size and weight, *but eventually put a stamp on it in order to save the trouble of weighing, and this stamp became the sign of its value."* *Aristotle's Politics,* 1–9.

It should be borne in mind, however, that all trade is barter, even when the precious metals are employed as intermediaries, the latter being articles of barter also, *possessing intrinsically the same value as the things for which they are exchanged.* The whole science of money hinges on this fact.

One commodity employed as money does not go out of use until it is superseded by another of superior qualifications for the service. This is the natural law that governs the change from one kind of money to another.

To give to coin all the elements of efficiency that it can possess, it is really only necessary to start it into circulation with its full weight and fineness of precious metal, that is, intrinsic equivalency, and its mintage or assay stamp, and let it go where it will. For examples, the Schlick Thaler of Bohemia; the Spanish milled dollar; Bechtler's gold coinage of the Carolinas ; the ingot of Moffatt & Company, and coins of Kellogg, Hewston & Company, of San Francisco; the Utah and Colorado gold coinages, and others. It is an advantage of a good standard, as gold or silver, that it may be used as a common measure of value, without altering very much the supply and demand of the article itself, so that the exchange value of the article may be wholly left to natural conditions. Here we have the natural law of metallic money in all its simplicity. The complexities are of our own making.

Debased money has entered into the experience of every civilized nation at some period of its history, and it is not necessary to particularize, but there are interesting chapters in Jacobs, showing conditions under Henry VIII. and Edward VI., and Macaulay, of a later date also, describing the imposition of brass money on Ireland, etc.

What I have designated as the natural law of money is inverted by the interjection of the legal-tender quality into money of unlimited issue; and what is commonly known as the Gresham Law demonstrates itself with certainty. Simply stated, this law is the operation of brokerage, assorting, culling, garbling, etc.,—thus always forcing the poorest money into circulation. And this all proceeds from the delusion on the part of men that, in some mystic or supernatural manner, governments can permanently regulate the value of money by conferring upon it a legal-tender quality. If by legislative enactment Government could exert that power, similar legislation would enable it to regulate the value of all commodities.

About 1366 Charles V., King of France, sometimes styled Charles the Wise, observing that the coins of the realm were in dire confusion, empowered one of his ministers, Nicholas Oresme, a man of distinguished attainments, a member of the French Imperial Government, and subsequently President of the College of

Navarre, to investigate and apply a remedy. As a result, Oresme published a treatise entitled, " A Theory of Money," and in this he outlined what is now called the Gresham Law. In 1526 Sigismund I. of Poland, to which Prussia then belonged, observing that the coins and money of his realm were in a deplorable condition of debasement, which was and had been the chronic condition of all Europe, selected Nicholas Copernicus, the great astronomer, to consider the subject; and Copernicus, after investigation, wrote a treatise setting forth doctrines that had been formulated one hundred and sixty years before by Oresme for the King of France, though there is no evidence to indicate that he knew the conclusions arrived at by Oresme. The doctrines of Oresme and Copernicus are substantially identical:

1.   That it is impossible for the law to regulate the value of the coins, *i. e.*, the purchasing power.

2.   That all the law can do is to maintain the coinage at a fixed denomination, weight and purity.

3.   That it is robbery for the law to change the denomination, diminish the weight, or debase the purity of the coinage.

4.   That it is impossible for good, full-weighted coin and debased coin to circulate together.

5.   That the coins of gold and silver must bear the same ratio to each other as the metals in bullion do in the market.

In 1558 Queen Elizabeth, discovering in her realm the same unfortunate conditions connected with the coins that had existed in France two hundred years before, and in Poland the previous generation,—especially produced in England by the repeated debasements that occurred under Henry VIII. and Edward VI.,—selected Sir Thomas Gresham, one of the most eminent men of the day, who, amongst other claims to distinction, possesses that of having founded the Royal Exchange of London ; and he, after a careful examination of the matter, reached the same conclusions that had in turn been reached by Oresme and Copernicus, known now as the Gresham Law, and which, as formulated to-day and accepted by economists and financiers the world over, is briefly expressed in the following terms :

When two coins of the same denomination, but differing in commercial value, are current in the same nation, that which has the least value will be kept in circulation and the other withdrawn from it as much as possible, and hoarded, melted down, or exported,—*in short, that bad money drives out good.*

It may be fairly stated that this fundamental law of money is found to hold universally true in all ages and countries, and has been recognized and acknowledged by learned men in all discussions on the subject. It applies in the following cases :

1. If the coinage consists of only a single metal, as in the early coinage of England, and clipped, degraded, and debased coins be allowed to pass current with good coin, all the good coin will disappear from circulation. It is either hoarded, melted down, or exported. All laws are ineffectual to prevent this; the clipped, degraded, and debased coin will alone remain current.

2. If coins of two kinds of metal, such as gold and silver, are allowed to pass current together in unlimited quantities, and *if a legal ratio is attempted to be enforced between them which differs from their relative value in the markets of the world*, the coin which is underrated disappears from circulation : it is either hoarded, melted down, or exported, and that which is overrated alone remains current. The law holds good also in relation to bank-note circulation.

3. This law is not confined to single and separate countries ; it is not limited in time or space ; it is absolutely universal. The Oresme, Copernicus, Gresham Law was expounded to the government of Great Britain by Locke, Newton, and other eminent men of the times ; but a knowledge of its workings did not reveal to them a remedy for continually existing and recurring evils of coinage, viz, the variations, the partings of the metals, the breakdown of parity of coin in circulation, etc., which were universal. A solution was found by Sir William Petty, who died in 1687, in a treatise of his discovered in 1691, viz, to make one metal the standard money, and the other subsidiary to it ; that so much subsidiary coin as could be kept in free circulation, redeemable in or exchangeable with the standard metal coins, was not only the best but the only method practicable for using both. That there could, of course, be no such thing as a double standard, and the greatest stability of money was to be attained by using one metal as standard. This theory was elaborated at a later date by Adam Smith.

It was the unbroken experience of centuries when Locke took up the question in England, as it has been the experience ever since, that immediately side by side with the legal ratio there is a market ratio, and there is no discernible tendency for the former to govern the latter.

The laws that finally govern finance are not made in conventions or congresses. The foundation of the international bimetallic theory—a purely empirical proposition—is thus erroneous from the beginning.

It is not claimed by any prominent advocates of bimetallism, for example Lavelleye of Belgium, Cernuschi of France, Ahrendt of Germany, Seyd (deceased), Gibbs and Helm of England, or Andrews or Walker of the United States, that the unrestricted free coinage of silver by any *one* government now maintaining a gold standard could be otherwise than disastrous. On the contrary, they declare in print that it would be calamitous, and that they do not desire to debase the standard of value: they would have every debt paid in gold, or its equivalent. And this is the attitude of bimetallists generally in Great Britain and Continental Europe. To all of which I remark: *When the two metals have unlimited free coinage at fixed ratios and are legal tender, the cheaper will, under all possible circumstances, drive the dearer out of circulation.*

Says Mr. Elijah Helm, one of the ablest bimetallists of England:

" The scheme put forward by bimetallists for the resuscitation of the joint standard by an international agreement is a new thing to the world. Nothing exactly like it has ever yet existed."

Says Prof. W. A. Shaw :

"The modern theory of bimetallism is almost the only instance in history of a theory growing, not out of practice, but of the failure of practice, resting not on data verified, but on data falsified and censure-marked. No words can be too strong of condemnation for the theorizing of the bimetallist who, by sheer imaginings, tries to justify theoretically what has failed in five centuries of history, and to expound theoretically what has proved itself incapable of solution save by cutting and casting away."

INTERNATIONAL BIMETALLISM.

M. BEERNAERT, the Minister of Finance of Belgium, opened the Brussels International Bimetallic Conference or Convention of December, 1892, as follows:

"The Conference in which you are called upon to take part has for its object the consideration of one of the most serious, complex and arduous problems presented to modern society. The subject of money touches all economic and social interests; it affects the commerce of the world, and is the real reason of more than one unexplained crisis," etc., etc.

There were proposals as early as the seventeenth century for a universal common ratio for the money metals, but there is no trace, in the writings of American statesmen, of the peculiar monetary theory on which bimetallism is now based. Probably there is no later exposition of the theory of international bimetallism than that contained in Prof. Nicholson's "Money and Monetary Problems," Mr. Elijah Helm's "Joint Standard," Archbishop Walsh's pamphlet of 1892, and Prof. E. B. Andrews' essays, published in book form in 1894, under the title of "An Honest Dollar," which, condensed, is Jevon's illustration of Wolloski's doctrine of two balancing hoards, based upon what is known as the quantitative theory of money, which proceeds on the assumption that there is a pool of money into which a balance of the precious metals falls after other uses have been satisfied, and that prices rise or fall proportionately with an increase or diminution of the pool, otherwise stated thus:

"Imagine two reservoirs of water, each subject to independent variations of supply and demand. In the absence of any connecting pipe, the level of the water in each reservoir will be subject to its own fluctuations only. But, if we open a connection, the water in both will assume a certain mean level, and the effects of any excessive supply or demand will be distributed over the whole area of both reservoirs, which enables one metal to take the place of the other as an unlimited legal tender."

This theory being based on the conception of governmental power: first, by Archbishop Walsh, that, "while legislation cannot directly give value to a thing, it can do so indirectly,—it can set up a demand which is one of the factors of value;" second, by Professor Andrews, that, "while law cannot control value independently of supply and demand, it can set free an economic force which will largely control supply and demand themselves."

"The bimetallist affirms: (1), that the monetary demand and supply of gold and silver, supposing both freely coined, in fixing the purchasing power of given quantities of them, overwhelmingly out-influence the commodity demand and supply; (2), that law can, at least, establish a legal-tender and debt-paying parity between a given quantity of gold and a given quantity of silver, which parity treaty could extend throughout any number of States; (3), that, since men are wont to discharge their pecuniary obligations as easily as they can, the existence of such legal-tender and debt-paying parity would, in case this legal parity should ever for any reason fail to match the commercial parity, stimulate the demand for the cheaper metal, appreciate it, and so tend to identify the parities again; (4), that if the field of legal parity is large, embracing in its bimetallic basin a third or even a quarter of the world's gold and silver, unless the value-ratio between the two metals denoted by the legal parity is widely at variance with the ratio in quantity between the total stocks of the two, the aforesaid stimulus of demand for the cheaper will overbear every tendency to part the parities named, and maintain the unit quantity of gold and the unit quantity of silver perpetually at the same value."

This reasoning seems to minimize the importance of the commercial demand for the precious metals for use in the arts *and as a commodity* in international commerce.

POSTULATE I.

" The bimetallist affirms that the monetary demand and supply of gold and silver, supposing both freely coined, in fixing the purchasing power of given quantities of them, overwhelmingly out-influence the commodity demand and supply."

The monetary demand is the demand upon the entire money mass, including not only money in all its various forms, but all the other signs of value and instrumentalities employed in effecting exchanges of which gold and silver constitute but a very small portion. The energy or pressure of this demand will be indicated only by the rates of interest, but will not in the slightest degree affect the purchasing power of money, or the commodity value of the material of which money is made.

From the days of Aristotle to the present time, it has been contended that coinage adds nothing to the value of the precious metals, but simply serves as a means of authentication by inspection only, and as a guarantee of the weight and fineness of the coin, and saves the trouble of weighing and assaying. It has simply the effect that the stamp of "Goldsmith's Hall" has upon spoons or plate, and adds no more to the value of the material of which metallic money is made than printing bank notes or bonds produces upon the market value of bank-note paper or parchment.

The fundamental error of this postulate, which goes to the very foundation of bimetallism, is that the coinage of gold and silver operates as a demand upon the metal mass, and, therefore, brings them, as commodities, within the general economic law of supply and demand. But this is a fatal error. The law of supply and demand, as applied to perishable commodities, is founded upon the theory that demand is the index of consumption, and that consumption, by the destruction or actual consuming of the material, creates a constant necessity for new supplies to satisfy new demands. But the precious metals, being practically imperishable and indestructible, are in no wise affected by mere coinage; but, upon the contrary, their condition is thereby greatly improved for employment in either the arts or international commerce, in which they are treated simply as commodities. Coinage, therefore, does not, in an economic sense, operate as consumption, but, upon the contrary, as a continual hoarding and stocking of the metal, the direct tendency of which is to depress its value as a commodity, by which alone its purchasing power as money is governed, and which will always be indicated by the true par of exchange, just as the demand for money will be indicated by the rates of interest. The facts, therefore, are just the reverse of those stated. Coinage exerts no influence whatever in fixing the purchasing power of the metals, which is governed entirely by the commodity demand and supply operating through the rates of international exchanges, which fix the commercial values.

POSTULATE 2.

No one will deny this proposition. But, unless the legal parity established conforms to the commercial parity, it can only be maintained under exclusive coinage for account of the Government, and not under free coinage. And even then it can only be maintained locally as a circulating medium, but not internationally as a medium of foreign exchange, which will always be based on the commercial parity.

POSTULATES 3 AND 4.

These practically rest on the same basis and involve the same error pointed out in No. 1, in assuming that "free coinage" is a demand upon the metal mass, whereas it is evidence of an absence of demand, as gold and silver go to the mint only because they will command no better price in the open market.

When the commercial and legal parities differ, however, while the difference may stimulate the demand for the cheaper metal for the purpose of coinage with a view of cheating creditors, it will produce no effect whatever in restoring the parity or equilibrium, for the reason given under Postulate No. 1.

The only experiment which history affords us of a practical test of this theory is the memorable one made by France from 1853 to 1859, the practical result of which was the very reverse of what is here claimed. Prior to 1853 the average price of silver for 30 years showed that at 15½ to 1 that metal was overvalued about 1¾ per cent, and France during that period had practically only a single standard of silver. But, in consequence of the great demand for that metal in London for Oriental account, its commercial parity rose above 15½, and an immense drain of silver from the Bank of France set in. To check this and restore the equilibrium, the bank went into the London market and paid $3,000,000 in premiums for gold in less than three years, which exceeded the disparity between the metals. For five years her coinage of gold averaged $90,000,000 per annum, or 80 per cent of the world's product, and yet gold declined over 1 per cent in value under this enormous coinage. But, to cap the climax, in 1859 she broke the world's record by coining $130,000,000 of gold, or $10,000,000 in excess of the entire product of the world, and yet the only effect was that gold fell 1 per cent lower. Or, in other words, silver had advanced over 2 per cent under this enormous coinage of the cheaper metal, the controlling factor being the rate of Oriental exchange on the London market, thus showing conclusively that coinage is utterly powerless, when brought in contact with the inexorable laws of commerce, to affect or change the parity between the metals; and this whole theory—the quantitative theory—lacks foundation in any known principle of economic law, and is a fallacy.

Again, I quote from Professor Andrews:

"Writers and thinkers of the highest ability believe that all necessary or attainable fixity of general prices is to come from international bimetallism. There can indeed be no doubt that this scheme would, for a long time, render extraordinary service, *if it could only be carried into effect.*"

So much for the bimetallist view. To restate the answer already given: Supposing that gold and silver are coined in unlimited quantities, and a fixed legal ratio is enacted between them.

1. Is it the fixed legal ratio enacted between the coins which governs the relative value of the metals in bullion?

2. Or, is it the relative value of the metals in bullion which governs the relative value of the coins?

3. And if it be found impossible for any single country to maintain gold and silver coined in unlimited quantities in circulation together at a fixed legal ratio, is it possible for any number of countries combined to do so by an international agreement?

It is not only my purpose to challenge the theory of international bimetallism,—which has been so ably done by scores of writers, notably of late by Giffen, MacLeod, Brough, Shaw, Laughlin, Wells, Leon Say, Beaulieu, Schoenhof and others,—but also to mention some of the fallacious reasons, inferences or conclusions advanced by its advocates, and to present their refutation. Here are specimens culled from Professor Andrews' utterances setting forth the evils of a gold standard, as, for example, the following at the Brussels Conference :

" They (the bimetallists) wish to stay that baneful, blighting, deadly fall in prices which for nearly thirty years has infected with miasma the economic life blood of the whole world."

And the following from his " An Honest Dollar :"

" The rise of gold, that is, the fall of prices, mainly consequent upon the demonetization of silver in and after 1873, has had, in particular, four great results, each of which has been pernicious in the extreme :

" First, it has tainted with injustice every time contract made anywhere in the gold-using world since 1873.

" Second, it has, all over this vast area, afflicted productive industry with anæmia, asphyxia and paralysis, owing to which the world's wealth is to-day less by billions than it would be had normal monetary conditions been enjoyed.

" Third, it has split the commercial earth in two, into a gold-employing and a silver-employing hemisphere, between which, so great is the difficulty of exchange, commerce has ceased to be a rational affair and has become in effect a game of hazard.

" And, fourth, by thus deranging the international exchange, it has discouraged, and, upon a colossal scale, lessened in amount the loaning of capital by rich countries to poor.

" I maintain it has been an absolute and unmitigated curse to human civilization."   *   *   *

However much a scarcity of gold may possibly have contributed to the recent fall of prices, and, through that, to the depression of trade,—which I do not admit,—it does not necessarily follow that the effect will be continued, nor that trade will be permanently contracted. A less number of gold and silver pieces at low prices of commodities will serve for the same exchanges as a larger number at higher prices. But the fundamental mistake of Prof. Andrews is in assuming that metallic money alone measures values,—influences prices. It is, if at all, the whole money fabric built upon metallic money that does so,—*Credit Money*—bills of exchange, bank notes, cheques, money orders, etc.—sustaining 98 per cent of the transactions of commerce. And, so long as these instruments are settled on a gold basis, they are gold measures of value. For example, let us take foreign commerce, aggregating say sixteen thousand millions of dollars per annum. Less than 2 per cent of gold is required to settle the balances of all this vast volume of trade, and therein credit represents confidence, the most important factor of all in the world's commercial relations. The New York Clearinghouse balances are not infrequently more in a week than the total current money of the United States.

Says Daniel Webster: "Credit has done more, a thousand times, to enrich nations than all the mines of all the world." To clear up the confusion of bimetallist perception, we have only to revert to the sound doctrine of the ancients,—that exchangeability is the sole essence and principle of wealth. Witness Demosthenes' dictum : "If you were ignorant of this, that credit is the greatest *capital* of all toward the acquisition of wealth, you would be utterly ignorant."

A point that the silver advocates leave out of consideration, but which will assert itself in monetary matters, is that the quantity of metallic money that can be got into *circulation* in any one country, or, for that matter, in the whole world, is limited. This is one of the stumbling blocks to the bimetallists. *This limitation arises because of the basic function of money. Metallic money is not in the main the value* FOR *which things are exchanged, but the value* BY *which they are exchanged*, ninety-eight per cent of the transactions of the world being effected by the signs and instrumentalities of metallic money.

" Metallic money, from the nature of its inherent value, unlike other forms of money founded upon mere credit, and which are mere signs, is an intrinsic equivalent, as well as a medium of exchange; and, therefore, the amount of such money which any nation will possess, or can retain in circulation, will bear just such a relation to the whole volume of metallic money in circulation among commercial nations as the surplus of its disposable products, which are measured by it, bears to those of other nations with whom it has commercial intercourse, and will, therefore, be precisely the same in amount whether the standard by which its exchangeable commodities are measured consists of a single metal or of two metals at a fixed ratio. By the operation of this law of exchangeable equivalents, the precious metals will always distribute themselves equitably among the nations of the earth in accordance with their respective standards of value and relative balances of trade."

It is not true that the quantity of money, apart from the possibly mischievous consequences of any sudden change, socially and otherwise, can affect materially the real wealth and welfare of an industrial community. As John Stuart Mill himself saw and expressly stated in a passage which is uniformly not quoted by the later adherents of the quantity theory :

" The proposition respecting the dependence of general prices upon the quantity of money in circulation must for the present be understood as applying only to a state of things in which money, that is, gold or silver, is the exclusive instrument of exchange, and actually passes from hand to hand at every purchase, credit in any of its shapes being unknown. When credit comes into play as a means of purchasing, distinct from money in hand, the connection between prices and the amount of the circulating medium is much less direct and intimate, and such connection as does exist no longer admits of so simple a mode of expression."

Mr. Giffen says :

" There is a relation between the quantity of standard money and prices, but it is rather one in which prices assist in determining the quantity of the precious metals to be used as money, and not one in which prices are themselves determined by that quantity. There are some complicated elements in the problem ; but this is the substantial result. Allowing for oscillations and exceptions, the chronic ratios of exchange between gold and silver and other commodities are not determined by any special qualities these metals have as money. It is the range of prices as part of a general economic condition which helps to determine the quantity of money in use, and not the quantity of money in use which determines the prices."

One word more of the international bimetallist. Not content with outdoing Jeremiah in their lamentations, some of them enter into judgment with all opposers. Said Mr. A. J. Balfour, of Manchester, England, three years ago, reiterated by Prof. Andrews, at Golden Gate Hall, in San Francisco, two years ago, " Any man who denies the entire feasibility of international bimetallism writes himself down as ignorant of the latest developments of economic science." This is simply

sound and fury, signifying nothing. He might just as
well have said, "Any man who denies the entire feasibility of an international agreement for the abolition
of war writes himself down as ignorant of the latest
development of altruistic feeling in the human race."
The first is not more likely than the second, and to see
how probable the latter is one has but to contemplate
the Armenian, Transvaal and Venezuela episodes.

Mr. Balfour was delivered of his rhetorical flight
when his party was out of power. When returned to
power his utterances indicated that the English poli-
tician is not essentially different from the American.
Approached by a bimetallist as to the probability of
action by the Conservative government in behalf of
bimetallism, he declared that his expressions of opinion
were simply his own and not binding upon any members of his party. When pressed to say whether any
government action would be taken in the interest of
bimetallism, he frankly declared there would not; that
he deemed it injudicious.

Archbishop Walsh, after writing a comparatively
plausible argument in behalf of international bimetallism, concludes with this piece of fiatism: "New
sovereigns might now be issued containing about one-
third the weight of gold less than in the sovereign
hitherto issued. Next year, in case of increase in
the value of gold contained, there might be a new
issue of sovereigns with a proportionately smaller
amount of gold," and so on *ad infinitum*. And Prof.
Andrews' doctrine is, in the last analysis, practically
the same, viz: When the need comes to change the
ratio do it by lightening the gold coins. Dr. Walsh's

argument, however, is simply a plea for Irish tenant farmers, and comes to this: " If the State is unable, or unwilling, to apply a radical remedy, by changing its currency system, out of which the existing evil— long-time land leases—has grown, it surely is bound, at the very least, to take in hand the readjustment of the terms of those obligations which, through the working of that system, have grown to be so oppressively burdensome."

Returning again to Prof. Andrews. It is, of course, possible, theoretically, that with international bimetallism the world's productivity since 1870 might have been greater than it has been,—just as John Stuart Mill raises the question of how much more civilized the world might be now if Christianity had been adopted by the Roman government under Marcus Aurelius, instead of one hundred and fifty years later, under Constantine ;—but it was not.

Some of the national steps for adopting gold as the standard of value, so far as expert or scientific consideration is concerned, have, approximately, been as follows: Prior to the year 1871, the countries that used the gold standard were Great Britain and her colonies, Portugal, Turkey, Brazil and the Argentine Republic,— Great Britain in 1816 (resumption of specie payments 1821),—though gold, because of its efficiency, had by choice been the money of commerce for a century previously. Of twenty powers represented at the International Monetary Convention at Paris, 1867, all (including the United States) favored the gold standard except Holland. France's movement really began in

1853–57, when she advantageously exchanged a large volume of silver, $300,000,000, for gold. The subject was discussed by Bosredon, Chevalier, Levasseur and other French economists, Levasseur declaring that gold had made itself the standard, and that France should make the law conform to the fact. In 1868 and 1869 two committees declared the superior efficiency of gold. The Imperial Commission of France, appointed in 1869, says: "On the general market, silver tends to depreciate, while gold is asked for. More than 500 millions in silver five-franc pieces are already accumulated at the Bank of France, and the public is no longer willing to receive these heavy pieces. Thus silver appears to be falling into disfavor, and we must hasten to demonetize it if we do not wish to be left the last to be encumbered with the inconvenient metal." The preamble of the French Currency Act of 1876 says: "From 1815 Great Britain has laid down principles which have attracted around her an ever-increasing circle of nations;" and, further, "From 1857 the French Government has studied the question, and it may be stated that since that date the principle of the gold standard has won increasing favor through our several administrations." The German economist, Dr. Soetbeer, began to discuss the question in 1863, and reported to a congress of German economists in 1868, upon which Germany decided, one year later, in favor of gold. The United States of America omitted the silver dollar from coinage in 1873, though it had not been in use for forty years. Holland adopted the gold standard in 1875; Denmark, Sweden and Norway entered a gold-standard union in 1876; and Finland adopted that standard in 1877. In 1873 Belgium suspended free coinage of silver; the other States of the Latin Union, France, Switzerland, Italy, etc., following in January, 1874; whereupon the *Economist Francaise* said : " It is a step toward the abolition of a law which, after seventy years' experience, had been found to be effete in theory and prejudicial in action." Russia discontinued free coinage of silver in 1876.

The report of the special commission of the upper house of Austro-Hungary said, 1879, that "It became clear, as long ago as the decade 1860–70, when Europe was becoming saturated with gold, that this was the only metal fitted to be the standard of nations of advanced civilization. Gold was dominant and the standard of value in all trade on a great scale as early as the fourteenth and fifteenth centuries, even though silver was then the standard in all domestic exchanges. In every age there is some metal dominant in the industry of the world, which forces its way with elemental strength in the face of any public regulation, and in our day gold is that metal." Italy limited silver coinage in 1883; Persia, Roumania, etc., later on, say 1887; later still, Chile. All this, too, despite the various monetary conventions: the United States Commission of 1876; the international (Paris) conventions of 1878 and 1881; the independent Paris convention in 1887; the Royal Commission (London), 1887; and the international convention (Brussels), 1892. Here, then, notwithstanding these six monetary congresses, within thirty years after France's conclusion that gold was the best standard of value, because of its greater stability, utility and efficiency, we see all the important Western powers, including the United States of America, Canada and Australia, on the gold-standard basis, that is to say, those peoples that transact more than 70 per cent of the commerce of the world, and whose governments control 70 per cent of the world's population. This cannot be regarded as caprice, or as the result of conspiracy, but is a natural gravitation toward greater efficiency in money. Says one of the best economic writers of to-day: "The gold standard has made its way in the world, not only without design on the part of individuals, but in spite of the strenuous resistance of almost all the men who busied themselves with the subject." So far as I have read, the changes have all been from silver to gold, and there is no case on record of a change from gold to silver. Whether these changes were wise or unwise, they were made, and the United States, alone and unaided, cannot undo them. "It is a condition and not a theory that confronts us."

If silver as standard money is now going out of use in a natural way we cannot stop it, and the attempt to do so can only involve us in trouble. Yet this movement —the supremacy of gold as the standard—within this century, particularly within this generation, or the past four decades, has been multifariously denounced as a demoniac crime against humanity,—Prof. Andrews himself, at Brussels, as already quoted, denouncing it as the cause of "the baneful, blighting, deadly fall in prices," etc.; that the fall in prices of commodities was caused by the action of the Powers in adopting the gold standard; and that all over this vast area (the gold-using world) it has afflicted productive industry with anæmia, asphyxia and paralysis; that it has been an absolute and unmitigated curse to human civilization ; that the world's wealth to-day is less by billions than it would be had what he calls normal monetary conditions been enjoyed.

Let us examine these extraordinary assertions. First, however, let me here call attention to the scant allusion in Professor Andrews' pages to two most important factors, which he has almost entirely ignored in the consideration of this question : The general financial collapses and industrial depressions and stagnations of 1815, 1826, 1837–41, 1848, 1857–61, 1865–66, 1873–77 and 1883–85, all of which affected Great Britain, France and the United States of America, save that of 1873–77, which France escaped by reason of the previous Franco-German war disaster. That of 1857–61 was a period in which primary money,—money of ultimate redemption,—silver as well as gold, was in full force and effect, and gold more plentiful throughout the world, comparatively speaking, than at any other period of history. Next, that the enjoyment by the laboring class (ninety-five persons out of every hundred) of wages on a gold basis, which have not fallen as compared with gold, *but have risen largely*, is, in degree of importance to interest on all forms of long-time obligations, at least as ten to one.

By reviewing a considerable period of time, especially in this century, we find that the general tendency is toward lower values ; and this applies not only to the precious metals, but to all products of man's labor. Since the introduction of steam-power machinery and subdivision of labor, the tendency toward lower prices has been more decided than before. To obtain a more abundant supply of the necessaries, comforts and luxuries of life is the object of all industry, and with the increase of supply comes the reduction in price. This is the natural order of progress, of civilization, and I offer the following statistics as a complete refutation of " anæmia, asphyxia and paralysis " in the industrial world.

No attempt is made in the following figures to be absolutely exact to a fraction. They are intended, however, to show by close approximation the general advance in the industrial and commercial world during the period treated of. It should be borne in mind that the natural increase of population is only a slight fraction over one per cent per annum.

Percentages of Increase in the Production, etc., of Articles in the United States, 1870–93.

Barley	165
Coal	400
Corn	50
Crops, cereal	123
Copper	1030
Cotton	213
Iron	328
Lead	859
Manufactures	276
Oats	158
Petroleum	860
Potatoes	60
Railroads, mileage	250
" capital and bonded debt	311
" earnings, gross	168
" earnings, net	51
Rye	73
Sugar	537
Steel	4628
Silver	200
Gold	41
Wheat	68

World.

Sugar 100
Gold 120
Silver (coinage value) approximately.................... 300
Coffee 260

Coffee shows an increased value of from 65 to 85 per cent, according to different reports upon same.

	1842.	1875.	1885.	1894.	1895.
Coffee, tons............	200,000	505,000	718,000	650,000	725,000
Total value of crop	....	....	....	$260,000,000	$255,000,000

Productions in the United States.

ARTICLE.	1870.	1880.	1890.	1893.	1895.
Barley, bushels.........................	29,761,305	44,113,495	63,000,000	69,869,000	87,072,744
Coal, tons	33,000,000	63,822,830	140,000,000	163,000,000	....
Copper, tons.............................	13,000	20,260	115,000	147,000	....
Corn, bushels...........................	760,944,549	1,754,861,535	1,489,970,000	1,619,496,131	2,151,138,580
" price per bushel	a92½c.	b50c.	b48c.	b50c.	b48c.
Crops, bushels...........................	1,377,477,432	2,686,145,028	2,503,853,000	2,750,905,856	3,556,967,806
Cotton, bales	3,154,346	5,757,397	7,313,726	6,717,142	9,892,776
Cut nails, cost per barrel............	$4.40	$3.68	$2.00	$1.44	$1.47
Iron, pig, tons...........................	1,665,179	3,840,000	9,202,793	7,124,501	9,446,308
" " price per ton	$33.25	$28.50	$18.40	$14.52	$13.10
Lead, tons................................	17,830	88,700	161,754	163,983	....
Oats, bushels.............................	282,107,157	407,858,900	523,621,000	638,854,000	824,443,537
" price per bushel	....	42.6c.	28.9c.	35.9c.	28.9c.
Petroleum, barrels......................	5,000,000	26,286,000	46,000,000	48,000,000	....
" price per barrel........	$3.86	94½c.	77c.	64c.	....
Potatoes, bushels.......................	114,975,000	....	....	183,034,000	297,237,370
Pensions, amount.......................	$27,780,811	$57,240,540	$106,493,890	$158,155,000	$140,959,361
Rye, bushels	16,918,795	19,831,595	28,000,000	26,555,000	27,210,070
Silver, production, ounces.........	13,000,000	30,320	54,500,000	60,000,000	....
Steel, tons................................	68,750	1,250,000	4,277,071	3,215,686	....
Steel rails, price per ton............	$106.75	$67.50	$31.75	$28.12	$24.33
Wheat, bushels................	287,745,626	459,479,503	399,262,000	396,131,725	467,102,947
" price per bushel	a$1.29	b$1.21	b98c.	b74c.	b67c.
Wool clip, pounds	162,000,000	232,500,000	276,000,000	303,000,000	294,296,000
Sugar, pounds....	178,304,592	207,877,278	497,169,856	463,268,627	729,392,561
" price per pound..............	12.6c.	8½c.	6¼ c.	4¾ c.	4½c.
" world production, tons...	2,738,000	3,670,000	5,500,000	6,547,615	7,291,500

a—Paper value.   b—Gold value.

Railroads in the United States.

	Miles.	Capital and funded debt.	Earnings, gross.	Earnings, net.	Dividends.
1871.....	52,920	2,644,627,645	403,329,209	141,746,404	56,456,681
1894.....	181,454	10,741,363,319	1,080,305,015	322,539,276	85,278,669

Or an increase in mileage of 250 per cent in 24 years.

1870........Total railway mileage of the world.........128,235
1894...... "   "   "   "   "   " 423,923

An increase of 231 per cent.

In the United States, railway mileage increased 250 per cent.
" " " capital and bonded debt " 311 "
" " " gross earnings, only " 168 "
" " " net earnings, " " 51 "

Here we see, in the item of capital and bonded debt, the pertinency of Professor Farnham's remarks in the *Yale Review* for August, 1895, as follows :

" When we consider the readiness with which new and hazardous enterprises are entered into, the large amount of business that is done on foreign capital, and the number of failures from insufficient capital, amounting in the United States to about one-third of the total number, it seems reasonable to hold that what this country needed was some check upon speculation quite as much as a stimulus."

Average freight rate per bushel of wheat for transportation from Chicago to New York :

	1870.	1893.	1895.
By lake and canal....	17.1 cents.	6.⅓ cents.	4.11 cents.
By lake and rail.....	22. "	8. "	6.95 "
By all rail..........	33.3 "	14.7 "	12.17 "

As to the Atlantic States railways we find the charges per ton per mile as follows :

	1868.		1892.	
The Boston & Albany R. R.............	28	mills.	16	mills.
The Fitchburg Ry. of Massachusetts......	48	"	9	"
The Vermont Central System..........	25	"	8	"
New York & New England Ry...........	64	"	12	"
New York, New Haven & Hartford.......	51	"	18	"
New York Central Ry..................	26	"	7	"
Lake Shore & Michigan Southern	24	"	6	"
Michigan Central......................	25	"	7	"
Cleveland, Cincinnati, Chicago & St. Louis..	19	"	7	"
	310	"	90	"

An average decrease for the 9 roads of 70 per cent.

To compare railroad freight rates,—through business,—Pacific System:

	1872.	1894.
Per ton per mile, east bound.	23 mills.	9 mills.
Per ton per mile, west bound.	25 "	8 "
Per ton per mile, local......	44 "	25 "
Passenger rates, all classes..	38 mills per mile.	19 mills per mile.

The Interstate Commerce Commission report to December 1, 1894:

Freight revenue per ton per mile, in cents or fractions of a thousand parts:

1888.	1889.	1890.	1891.	1892.	1893.	1894.
1.001	.922	.941	.895	.898	.878	.866

A reduction in seven years of 14 per cent.

Passenger revenue per passenger per mile, in cents or fractions of a thousand parts:

1888.	1889.	1890.	1891.	1892.	1893.	1894.
2.349	2.165	2.167	2.142	2.126	2.108	1.976

A reduction in seven years of 16 per cent.

Mulhall, in the *North American Review* for June, 1895, mentions that freight charges in the United States in 1890 averaged 93 cents (interstate commerce 94 cents) per ton per hundred miles, which is less than half the charge ($1.90) now prevailing in Europe, and less than half the charge prevailing in the United States twenty years ago. The difference between the present rates in the United States and Europe implies a saving in this respect alone of $845,000,000 yearly to the American people, or 10 per cent on the original cost of constructing the lines. Does anybody consider this fall in rates a " baneful, blighting, deadly " influence upon the interests of the people ?

Savings Banks.

Up to 1870 the savings bank deposits of the United States reported were................................. $ 549,874,358
In 1887 they reached......................... 967,000,000
In 1893 they reached........................ 1,809,000,000

Total resources of such banks, deposits, surplus and capital represented :

In 1882....................................$1,053,000,000
In 1893.................................... 2,014,000,000

National Banks, United States.

	Capital.	Net earnings.	Per cent.
1873	$488,100,951	$65,048,578	13.3
1891	760,108,201	75,763,514	9.9

In the days of Charles and Cromwell rates of interest in England were 10 per cent. At present a 2¾ per cent interest-bearing consol sells above par ; and a gold-bearing 3 per cent United States bond will sell above par. The rate of dividend interest in California savings banks has fallen from 10 per cent in 1870 to 4 per cent in 1895. In the Atlantic States, say New England and New York, it has fallen from 6 per cent in 1870 to 4 and 3½ per cent in 1895.

Money in the United States.

1873..... Money per capita, $18.58—chiefly irredeemable paper.
1891..... Money per capita, 34.31
1896..... Money per capita, 31.20

1873..Circulation per capita, \$18.04—chiefly irredeemable paper.
1891..Circulation per capita, 23.41
1896..Circulation per capita, 22.47

Wealth, United States.

1860 ....\$16,000,000,000
1870 28,000,000,000
1880 45,000,000,000
1890 65,000,000,000

In 1890 the richest country in the world.

This extraordinary increase may be discounted somewhat because of the crude method of earlier censuses.

Wealth of Great Britain, France, Spain, United States of America, Australia, Tasmania and New Zealand and Canada combined, estimated :

1870 ....\$100,000,000,000
1890 200,000,000,000

Gold, World.	Silver, World.
	(Commercial Value.)
1853............\$155,000,000	
1870............ 107,000,000	1870............\$ 51,575,000
1874............ 91,000,000	1880............ 85,636,000
1890............ 120,000,000	*1890............ 172,235,000
1894............ 180,000,000	1894............ 105,757,300
1895............ 200,000,000	1895............ 110,000,000

Present annual output of gold alone is more than annual output of gold and silver together thirty years ago.

Estimate of world's stock of *coin* (U. S. Mint Report, 1894) :

1860 ....\$3,900,000,000
1894 8,021,000,000
1896 8,300,000,000

One of Professor Andrews' wails is that " Nations in the gold group can no longer trade freely with those in the silver group." The movement of merchandise and silver in connection with India has been as follows :

---

* The price of silver was speculatively inflated in 1890, owing to pending legislation by the United States of America, the result of which was a dismal failure.

Shipments of Bullion and Specie from European Money Centers to Eastern Countries. (Including Sundry and Alexandria, to 1886.):		Statement of Yearly Tonnage Passing Through the Suez Canal from its Opening up to 1894:
18,168,303	1862	
21,455,884	1863	
24,318,189	1864	
13,933,183	1865	
10,032,626	1866	
3,659,154	1867	
10,189,904	1868	
9,053,186	1869	
110,810,389		
4,507,388	1870	436,699
8,687,431	1871	761,467
10,988,705	1872	1,160,743
7,807,605	1873	1,367,767
11,448,512	1874	1,631,650
6,303,700	1875	2,009,984
15,147,012	1876	2,096,771
20,588,599	1877	2,355,447
85,478,952		**11,820,438**
8,403,350	1878	2,269,678
13,391,086	1879	2,263,332
10,983,339	1880	3,057,421
7,985,996	1881	4,136,779
13,829,591	1882	5,074,808
10,100,591	1883	5,775,861
14,040,596	1884	5,871,500
13,365,500	1885	6,335,752
92,100,049		**34,885,131**
7,572,596	1886	5,767,655
8,541,505	1887	5,903,024
7,118,243	1888	6,640,834
11,380,823	1889	6,783,187
11,507,122	1890	6,890,094
8,809,828	1891	8,698,777
12,317,887	1892	7,712,028
14,667,799	1893	7,659,068
81,915,803		**56,054,667**
10,357,302	1894	8,039,175

Yearly tonnage passing through the Suez Canal was:

In 1870.. 436,609 tons

In 1894........................... ....8,039,175 "

The foreign trade of India has more than doubled since 1872, and even the Lancashire manufacturers, who complain so bitterly, have more than doubled their exports of cotton goods to India. The quantity of cotton cloth exported to India in the year 1873 was 990 millions of yards; while in 1894 the total had risen to the enormous amount of 2,279 millions of yards. The Secretary of the Lancashire Cotton Spinners' and Manufacturers' Association finds, on investigation of the facts, that while silver countries have, since 1873, increased their consumption of English cotton cloth by 100 per cent, gold countries have only increased it by 17 per cent, and India has, notwithstanding the increase in Indian mills, increased its consumption of English cotton manufactures by 130 per cent.

In regard to the increase of wages on a gold basis, Prof. Andrews uses the following language : " The average value of labor, including unskilled, has not, in my belief, advanced so much as gold, even if it has risen at all." Rogers' " Economic Interpretation of History;" McKenzie's " History of the Nineteenth Century;" Walter Besant's " Fifty Years Ago;" the report of Robert Giffen to the British Parliament on the progress of the working classes ; one by Alfred Neymark to the Statistical Society of Paris ; Guyot's " Economic Science;" D'Avenal's " History Economique," as shown in Schoenhof's " History of Money and Prices;" McMasters' " History of the American People ; " C. C. Jackson's " Has Gold Appreciated ; " the United States Senate Committee Report, commonly called the "Aldrich Report on Prices, Wages and Transportation," the latter work a monument of industry, patience and intelligence, and other literature on the subject too numerous to mention, all show that wages have increased in fifty years under the gold standard approximately over 60 per cent, and during this century 100 per cent. After examining the Aldrich Report, Prof. Taussig said: "All in all, the figures show that the purchasing power of money wages has been rising steadily for at least twenty years, and that the decline in prices since 1873, and especially since 1882, has been a source of prosperity, and not of depression, to the community at large." As to what has been the result to wage-earners under the gold standard in this country, I submit the following conclusions from the same Report:

Prices and wages were examined from 1840 to 1892. The evidence demonstrated beyond all controversy two facts: (1) that wages, measured by the best dollar, had been increasing all the time; (2) that prices, measured by the same standard, were falling during the whole fifty-two years. This is a happy condition for the wage-earner. He is doubly benefited by the standard of the gold dollar. He is benefited by the constant increase of his daily wage, and again by the constant decline in the prices of the things which he must buy. From 1840 to 1892 the rate of wages increased in the United States over 60 per cent, while the prices of things he had to buy were constantly declining. The investigation covered the prices of 223 articles, which showed an average reduction of 25 per cent. Many of the articles, which were every-day necessaries of life, declined much more than that. Fuel fell 75 per cent, metal 39, drugs and medicines 39, and house-furnishing goods 40 per cent. This is to-day the wage-workers' situation on a gold standard. Let us compare it with the paper-standard era, when the country had the highest prices it has ever known.

In 1866 the unlimited issue of paper money had banished gold from our circulation, and the paper dollar was the standard. Wages in paper money had risen 52 per cent above the gold rate of 1860.

At the same time we find that beef had risen 108 per cent above the gold rate, hams 198 per cent, New Orleans molasses 135 per cent, rice 182 per cent, salt 102 per cent, refined sugar 85 per cent, calico 121 per cent, ingrain carpets 141 per cent, denims 274 per cent, drillings 265 per cent, sheeting 291 per cent, shirting 222 per cent, coal 201 per cent, nails 132 per cent, pine shingles 121 per cent, window 'glass 10 x 14, 126 per cent, and quinine 131 per cent. Here we see that a depreciated standard of value robbed wage-earners of more than half their earnings. Of all the contrivances for cheating the laboring classes of mankind, none is more effectual than a currency that is not convertible into metallic money of intrinsic equivalency.

I appreciate that estimating total relative prices without regard to relative importance or consumption of commodities is misleading, and in an analysis of such data, grouped according to relative importance of commodities, it showed that the fall in prices was 6 per cent less than otherwise shown. That is to say, taking 100 as a standard of average from the years of 1865 to 1869, the fall from 1870 to 1885 was 24 per cent, as against 30 per cent where the relative importance of commodities was not considered. Eleven leading products of farms in the United States fell 26 per cent.

Prices.

	1873.	1891.	Per cent.	
Print cloth, per yard................$	.066	$ .029	56	
Quinine, per ounce................	2.65	.30	89	
Goblets, per dozen................	.85	.25	70	
10 x 14 glass......................	3.40	1.70	50	
Undershirts.......	1.41	.62	56	
Ginghams, per yard..............	.13	.06	54	
Carpets, two-ply ingrain, per yard..	1.14	.50	56	
Black pepper, per pound..........	.19	.09	53	
Molasses, per gallon..............	.69	.32	53	
Freight rate, per ton..............	2.00	.92	54	
Refined sugar, per pound..........	.116	.057	50	
Cut nails, per pound	.049	.016	62	
Pig iron, per ton..................	42.75	17.50	60	
Cotton, per pound................	.188	.10	53	⎫
Corn, per bushel..................	.61	.57	6	⎪
Wheat, per bushel................	1.31	.93	30	⎪
Bacon and hams, per pound.......	.088	.076	14	⎪
Lard, per pound................	.092	.069	25	Average
Pork, per pound	.078	.059	24	fall of 26
Beef, per pound..................	.077	.056	27	per cent.
Butter, per pound................	.211	.145	32	⎪
Cheese, per pound................	.131	.09	31	⎪
Tobacco, per pound..	.107	.087	19	⎪
Eggs, per dozen.................	.26	.17	35	⎭
Leather, per pound...............	.253	.16	36	
Starch, per pound................	.053	.032	40	
Illuminating oils, per gallon.......	.235	.07	70	
Steel rails, per ton	120.50	29.92	75	
Rio coffee, per pound.............	.18	.16	11	
Tea, per pound	.95	.25	73	
Sheeting, per yard...	.133	.068	48	
Drilling, per yard................	.141	.064	55	
Shirting, per yard................	.194	.106	45	
Standard prints..................	.113	.06	47	

Average reduction in eleven chief farm products, 26 per cent. Average reduction in twenty-three other products, 55 per cent.

According to Dr. Kral's tables for Hamburg, without going into details, the average of prices of all vegetables and animal food was considerably higher in 1884 than it was in 1844,—forty years previously.

Relative wages and prices in gold in the United States of all occupations, taking wages of 1860 as 100:

	Prices.	Wages.		Prices.	Wages.
1840	116.8	87.7	1871	122.9	147.8
1850	102.3	92.7	1880	106.9	141.5
1860	100	100	1890	92.3	158.9
1870	117.3	133.7	1891	92.2	160.7

The latest data obtainable shows that the annual average money wages of manual laborers in Great Britain increased from £43 8s. in 1876 to £53 16s. in 1892, or over 23 per cent in fifteen years, though this may have been partly due to restrictions on child labor; but the increase from 1845 to 1895 has been relatively as great as in the United States.

According to investigations of Yves Guyot, also J. B. Say, separately, the increase of wages in France from 1805 to 1883 was, in a superficial average upon ten callings, such as day laborers, cellar diggers, stonecutters, brickmasons, carpenters, blacksmiths, etc., 120 per cent; and the greatest advance in one of the five divisions of time into which this period was classified was in that from 1875 to 1883, the wages of carpenters and laborers having increased over 33 per cent and those of cabinet makers 50 per cent within that brief period, at the very time when, according to bimetallists' theories, wages ought to have fallen.

If a day's labor be a reasonable unit of value, as some economists, even Adam Smith, have contended, it is certain that, judged by that standard, gold has not risen. I assert that *the facts* submitted utterly disprove Professor Andrews' contention of "anæmia, asphyxia and paralysis." This country is not so much in need of more money as it is of more common sense and less hysteria.

To answer upon a historic basis the theories of the international bimetallists, it is enough to say that no form of bimetallism by which the two metals were coined without limit and were legal tender has ever succeeded. This is the unvarying verdict of history. For six hundred years, that is to say, since Florence began the minting of gold florins in 1252, which quickly extended to France, Flanders, Germany, and, later, to England, there have been a succession of reratings throughout the entire world in the endeavor to keep the two metals together, and fluctuations of less than one per cent in the difference between the commercial value and the coinage value of each have always been sufficient to exclude the more valuable from circulation; and, under present facilities of communication and exchange, one-fourth of one per cent would be sufficient to produce the same effect.

In the *Overland Monthly* for the present month of February, in an article on "Hard Times," Irving M. Scott says:

"Europe, from early times down to a late date, employed both gold and silver as the 'standard of value.' This country, in its colonial and confederate conditions, did the same. The United States, from the foundation of the Government (constitutional) down to 1873, employed both gold and silver, in accord with an Act of Congress making the standard unit of value 'One Dollar,' of a certain fineness. Thus, from 1687 to 1873, embracing a period of 186 years, our country employed both the silver dollar and the gold dollar— equal one to the other—as the standard unit of value and as redemption money. *Thus it is seen that from time immemorial gold and silver worked together harmoniously. A greater production of one or the other did not affect the parity established between them.*"

The closing assertion by a business man of Mr. Scott's standing is astonishing, for the facts are exactly the opposite. Among the ancient Phœnicians silver and gold circulated 1 to 1,—weight for weight. In India, at the time of Alexander's invasion, silver to gold was as 2 to 1, but in consequence of the rapid extension of commerce the ratio soon reached 6 to 1. In Athens, at the zenith of her power, the ratio at one time reached 13 to 1. At a little earlier period the ratio with the Romans was 10 to 1. They allowed the Æolians to pay their annual tribute in either silver or gold at this ratio. Between the fifth and thirteenth centuries, the great national formative period, gold was hoarded, and, though Byzantine, Arabian, Egyptian and Spanish-Moorish gold coins were to be found in circulation occasionally, there was no gold coinage by Western Europe until the close of the twelfth or the beginning of the thirteenth century, the impetus having been given by the Crusaders. There never was agreement in the thirteenth, fourteenth or fifteenth centuries, and the

sudden yield of money metals by the New World
utterly upset the mintage ratios of all Europe
during the sixteenth and seventeenth centuries.
There never was anything like an equal and
generally recognized ratio of value between gold
and silver prevailing at any single point of time.
At one and the same date a ratio of 7 or 8 to 1
prevailed in the Moorish parts of Spain, and 12 to 1
in the Christian parts (the kingdom of Castile).
Similarly, at a later period, in 1474, the ratio in
England was 11.15; in Germany 11.12 ; in France
11.00 ; in Italy 10.58; and in Spain 9.20. Vasco de
Gama found the ratio prevailing in South America
with the Indians 8 to 1. Changes of ratio in Europe
under the influence of New World metallic product are
indicated by the following figures:

1545–60	11.30 to 1	1621–40	14.00 to 1
1561–80	11.50 to 1	1641–60	14.50 to 1
1581–1600	11.80 to 1	1661	15.00 to 1
1601–20	12.25 to 1		

Or from 1545 to 1660, a period of 115 years, the ratios
of the two metals varied 33 per cent. And it is
reasonably certain that all important monetary transactions in England prior to the Elizabethan reformation of the coinage, under Gresham, were settled by
weight and not by tale.

Lord Liverpool, writing in 1805, says:

" The price of silver in dollars has varied in twenty-
three years,—that is, from the end of the year 1774 to
the 31st of December, 1797,—12 per cent (in round
figures), and even in the course of one year, that of
1797, no less than 9½ per cent. The variation in
the price of silver bullion appears to have been still

greater, by another account, with which I have been favored, by the later Mr. Garbett, an eminent merchant and manufacturer at Birmingham; it there appears that silver purchased by him, as a refiner, varied, according to his calculation, in the course of ten years, to 1793, more than 19¼ per cent, and in one year alone more than 13⅓ per cent."

In the 500 years, from the fourteenth to the eighteenth centuries inclusive, there were over 400 changes or reratings throughout Continental Europe; and even a cursory knowledge of the history of coinage of the last 500 years in the world will show that not alone has bimetallism, with free coinage, failed in Europe, but it failed also in India; that two distinct attempts were made there, both of which resulted disastrously. The difficult character of the question, as well as the nature of money dealings in the past, is well illustrated in a few words taken from Mr. D'Avenal, the French author of "Economic History," as interpreted by Mr. Schoenhof. Writing of former times, he says:

"An endless number of disks of gold, silver and billon were coined by all sorts of people in all kinds of countries, and these people had to value in livres, sous and deniers, at their true valuation, *by weight and fineness*. The barons and prelates who coined money regularly in the thirteenth century numbered eighty. There were consequently eighty coining standards, but in reality there were a good many more. Besides this, there were quite a number of pieces circulating of much more ancient date."

This author also pertinently remarks that "the current value of money does not obey the ordinances of kings," that is, legal enactment, government fiat.

Apart altogether from the arbitrary debasement of the coin, apart even from the changes of the ratio enacted with the mere crafty design of inducing a flow of gold, the monetary systems of the times were so rough, so unscientific, the tariffing of the coins of different nations against each other so inexact, of so hasty average, that it was simply impossible to provide general tables of equivalents of coins. The mint conventions of contiguous States in Europe in the sixteenth century were so frequent that their history has been characterized as a jungle of intricacies. A modern writer has said that to pick out and enumerate all the changes of ratings in Europe in a period of 600 years—the thirteenth to the eighteenth centuries inclusive—would be like counting the stars in the Milky Way. And in France, the criterion of the silverites, there were 150 changes in less than that number of years in the fifteenth and sixteenth centuries. During the French Revolution the ratings of gold and silver were changed over sixty times, with no effect whatever save to cheat the people. In that country, from 1820 to 1850, silver expelled gold, achieving a proportion as currency of 91 to 9, while gold only was in effective circulation from 1850 to 1873. Said the Chevalier Baisse, in his "Problem of Gold," written in 1859:

" A change of 1½ per cent in favor of gold sufficed, thirty or forty years ago, to cause that metal to disappear wholly from commercial payments. Under the *regime* of the law of the 7th Germinal, year XI (1803), gold had ceased to figure in transactions of any magnitude since it had acquired an appreciable premium. People took their gold to the money changer in order to pocket the premium, and made payments exclusively in silver, as every investigator knows."

Gold and silver never have at any time or place circulated freely, concurrently and indiscriminately *as legal-tender coins* at fixed ratios under unrestricted coinage.

It was the unbroken experience of centuries when Locke took up the question in England, as it has been the experience ever since, that side by side with the legal ratio there is immediately a market ratio, and there is no discernible tendency for the former to govern the latter. The laws that finally govern finance are not made in conventions or congresses. The foundation of the bimetallic idea is thus erroneous from the beginning, and there is no discoverer or great economist to set against the chain of authorities by which the opposite system has been established.

Locke gave, as sufficient reason why silver was then the best money of account, that the world had so decided,—that the world of commerce had so decided,—and that it is enough that the world had agreed on it and made it their common money. And this is sufficient reason to-day why gold is the standard money,—money of ultimate redemption with Western nations,—because all the progressive nations of the world have made it so, and that out of regard to its superior efficiency.

I would not have my hearers assume that scientists or economists, because they are ancient, are necessarily to be deemed infallible. About the last of the sixteenth century, Davanzate said: "All commodities which serve to satisfy the wants of man are by convention equal in value to all the gold, silver and copper." It would seem incredible that such an idea could have been entertained, yet it must have been, for Montesquieu appears to have adopted it, because Chevalier took the trouble to refute it as coming from him by simply pointing out that the money quantities of France were estimated at 3½ milliards of francs in value, while the value of real property alone amounted to 83 milliards of francs.

We have spoken of the Oresme, Copernicus, Gresham Law, which was expounded by Locke, Newton and other eminent men of the times to the government of Great Britain, but a knowledge of its workings did not reveal to them a remedy for continually recurring evils of coinage, viz, the variations, the parting of the metals, the breakdown of parity of coin in circulation, etc., which was universal. The remedy was not perceived even by the great expounders of the Gresham Law. A solution was found by Sir William Petty, who died in 1687, in a treatise of his discovered in 1691, viz, *to make one metal the standard money, and the other subsidiary to it; that so much subsidiary coin as could be kept in free circulation, redeemable in or exchangeable with the standard metal coin, was not only the best but the only method practicable for using both*. That there could, of course, be no such thing as a double standard, and the greatest stability of money was to be attained by using one metal as standard. This theory was elaborated at a later date by Adam Smith.

The best brief exposition extant of money on this basis —the Gresham-Petty laws—is by Lord Liverpool, at the beginning of this century,—say about 1805,—as follows:

" The standard coin of a country is the measure by which the value of all things bought and sold is regulated and ascertained, and it is itself, at the same time, the value or equivalent for which goods are exchanged, and in which contracts are generally made payable. In this last respect the standard coin, as a measure, differs from all others, and to the combination of the two qualities before defined, which constitute the essence of this standard coin, the principal difficulties that attend it in speculation and practice, both as a measure and an equivalent, are to be ascribed. These two qualities can never be brought perfectly to unite and agree ; for if the standard coin were a measure alone, and made, like all other measures, of a material of little or no value, it would not answer the purpose of an equivalent. And if it is made, in order to answer the purpose of an equivalent, of a material of value, subject to frequent variations, according to the price at which such material sells at the market, it fails on that account in the quality of a standard or measure, and will not continue to be perfectly uniform and at all times the same. Civilized nations have generally adopted gold and silver as the material of their standard coin, because these metals are costly and difficult to procure, little subject to variation in value, durable, divisible, and easily stamped or marked."

Lord Liverpool was not insensible to the possibility of a change in the value of a money metal in respect of itself, and that the standard metal might so vary ; but he held this difficulty to be so essentially inherent as not to be susceptible of remedy.

Following the teachings of Gresham, Locke, Newton and Petty, Great Britain, after the most careful consideration, and after centuries of monetary welter, decided in 1816 to legally adopt the gold standard, though, as already stated, because of its efficiency, gold had really been, through the custom and usage of merchants as well as by proclamation, the money of commerce for one hundred years previously. The master of the mint declared in 1816 that the law merely established and legalized the system which had been adopted by public opinion since 1717. So, also, the Acts of the United States Congress of 1853 and 1873 merely carried into full legal effect the Acts of 1834–37, a fact of nearly forty years.

As already stated, there is not a trace in the writings of American statesmen of the peculiar monetary theory on which bimetallism is now based. The conclusion that commodity values absolutely rule coinage values—purchasing power—was concurred in and accepted by the statesmen of our own country,—Morris, Gallatin, Hamilton, Madison, Jay, Jefferson, and other founders of our American Republic, and, later on, Webster, Clay, Jackson, Benton, Tilden, Cleveland, and others. Jefferson said, among other and similar utterances on the subject: " Just principles lead us to disregard legal proportions altogether, to inquire into the market price of gold in the several countries with which we shall be principally connected in commerce, and to take an average from them." This conclusion was followed in 1834 by the United States, as indicated by the following, taken from the Report of Currency Committee to Congress, June 30, 1832 :

" The Committee think that the desideratum in the monetary system is the standard of uniform value. They cannot ascertain that both metals have ever circulated simultaneously, concurrently and indiscriminately in any country where there are banks or money dealers; and they entertain the conviction that the nearest approach to an invariable standard is its establishment *in one metal*, which metal shall compose exclusively the currency for large payments,"—that is to say, standard money,—money of commerce, money of ultimate redemption. This conclusion is impregnable.

The only rational bimetallism possible is the circulation of so much silver as may be kept freely interchangeable with gold and as may be necessary for the minor transactions of trade. All silver hoarded by Government in excess of this means the withdrawal of just so much capital from active operations in the hands of the people,—for illustration, the present monetary status in the United States, which is a perverted example of the bimetallism of Sir William Petty. To assure the use of gold and silver at the same time on a par, gold *must* be the standard, and the coinage of silver so limited that the Government can maintain their exchangeability. And under such a policy any excess of silver beyond the actual uses of it by the people is, as stated above, just so much capital withdrawn from active operations, because the excess is useless for purposes of redemption and is a menace to the redemption money. If the coinage cannot be circulated, then it is waste to lock it up and circulate the paper instead, entailing all the disadvantages of paper without the advantage of its economy. The excess of silver over what can be practically used in active circulation is not more defensible than the Populists' farm-product Sub-Treasury schemes. The important point here is, that with all the complexity and confusion originating in notions of making money abundant (which will be referred to later on under the head of " CURRENCY "), our Government has arrived at nothing and has effected nothing which might not have been effected better by a thoroughly monometallic system, with gold for the standard.

" While it is admitted that no single nation can, by a legal-tender law, make a money buy more in the market than it is worth as property, it is asserted that an agreement among the nations having commercial relations to make depreciated silver full legal tender at an universally uniform ratio would put it on a par with gold in the markets of the world. Then would fifty cents' worth of silver, coined in a dollar piece, buy an hundred cents' worth of gold or of any other property. Such an agreement and its accompanying legislation would be absolutely barren and powerless to effect the proposed result, because trade alone fixes values, and nations as nations do not trade with each other. Governments are not traders. They are not in commerce. They neither buy nor sell. Their individual citizens trade with each other according to the unchanging element of human interest. The government of each furnishes protection and facilities for trade to its merchants, its selling producers and its buying consumers. But governments themselves are not merchants. They do not own the exchangeable properties of their citizens. They do not bargain them away. They have nothing to do with their price. They have nothing to do with what is taken in exchange for them, nor with the rate at which one is exchanged for the other. They keep the peace, protect property, administer justice, make it safe and convenient for their merchants and their customers to deal with each other within their several jurisdictions, enforce for them their lawful contracts, and there they stop. They are no part of the world of trade. They can, each within its own territory, rob creditors by legal-tender acts which are false to the facts and ethics of trade, and so drive away capital; but they can no more change the exchangeable value or commercial function of the money of trade than they can change the exchangeable ratios of cotton, hay, iron, cows, steamships, or any other form of property in which men deal with each other according to their needs and their mutual agreement upon values. If they could, all they would have to do to secure eternal commercial tranquillity would be to enact all forms of property to be money, all unlimited legal tender, fix their ratios to each other once for all, and then let the world run."

It is as impossible for the whole world, by international agreement, to maintain coins of two or more metals in circulation, in unlimited quantities, at a fixed legal ratio, differing from the relative natural or market value of the metals of which they are composed, as it is for separate and independent nationalities to do it, and the latter never has been done.

Let us now consider the status of the international bimetallic movement after twenty years of agitation. At the Brussels Convention of 1892 the delegates of the United States were, under date of November 22, 1892, thus instructed by Secretary of State John W. Foster:

" *You should not lose sight of the fact that no arrange-ment will be acceptable to the people or satisfactory to the Government of the United States which would, by any possibility, place this country on a silver basis while European countries maintain the single gold standard.*"

The British delegates asserted from the outset that they would not adopt bimetallism on the basis of free coinage; Germany and Austro-Hungary let it be known that they would not,—at least not without the con-currence of Great Britain; France explicitly declared this to be her attitude; and Weber for Belgium, Forssell for Scandinavia, and Raffalovich and De Thoener for Russia, declared that, in the years that had elapsed since former conventions,—1878, 1881,—they had seen no reasons for changing their convictions against it, citing examples to show how utterly impossible it is, in monetary matters, to resist natural forces by statutory laws or agreements. Forssell of Sweden voiced similar sentiments with a force and originality of reasoning, a wealth of learning and illustration, and a caustic wit, not exceeded by any member of the convention. Said Forssell: " The question is, What should be the size of a hogshead to contain a certain quantity of liquid when there is no possibility of stopping the bunghole?" And, further, " If the conference of Brussels contributes to establish and fortify the conviction that an interna-tional agreement for the free and unlimited coinage of silver is not only rejected for the moment, but is inadmissible for the future, it will have reached a very important result."

So the Brussels Convention closed with the following glittering generality in the way of a resolution,—a diplomatic courtesy of Baron de Renzis, the Italian delegate, who represented the Latin Union, in the absence of Mr. Tirard, French delegate:

"The International Monetary Conference, recognizing the great value of the arguments which have been developed in the reports presented and in the discussions at the meetings, and reserving its final judgment upon the subjects proposed for its examination, expresses its gratitude to the Government of the United States for having furnished an opportunity for a fresh study of the present condition of silver.

"The conference suspends its labors and decides, should the governments approve, to meet again the 30th of May, 1893. It expresses the hope that during the interval the careful study of the documents submitted to the conference will have permitted the discovery of an equitable basis for an agreement which shall not infringe in any way the fundamental principles of the monetary policy of the different countries."

But the real status had been previously expressed by Mr. Tirard in the Convention, and, as France is constantly cited by the silver agitators, I ask my hearers' indulgence for quoting at some length Mr. Tirard, then Minister of Finance of the French Republic and Governor of the Bank of France. Said Mr. Tirard:

"Gentlemen, I believe that if a conclusion could not be reached which would be accepted by everybody, or at least by a majority sufficient to establish the base of an international system, it is because the adoption would result necessarily, for several large States, in a radical change of their monetary legislation.

"That is, in truth, a difficult undertaking. Peoples already far advanced in civilization have habits, customs and laws which are adapted to their traditions. They are not applied in an arbitrary fashion ; they are bound up with the very conditions of the existence of these peoples.

" *Despite all the demonstrations and the speeches, all the publications, and all the newspaper articles, do we see the Powers named, and, too, others, change their opinion ?* NOT THE LEAST IN THE WORLD.

" Since the first day, we have heard upon this point declarations which were perfectly frank and sincere, declarations for which I, on my part, am grateful to their authors, because it is well to know upon what we may rely. We have heard the Minister of Germany, and the Minister of Austro-Hungary, and then Sir Rivers Wilson, declare that neither Germany nor Austro-Hungary nor England had any intention of modifying their monetary systems, with which they declared themselves fully satisfied. Under these conditions we evidently cannot re-establish free coinage, and I have not the vanity to believe that I should succeed in persuading the governments of these great countries, and their eminent representatives, that they are mistaken, that they have taken the wrong road, and that they are in error in remaining attached to gold monometallism. I consider, therefore, until some change takes place, that the question of free coinage is decided so far as we are concerned."

Said Mr. Currie, for Great Britain :

" After the repeated declarations of the delegates of France, Germany and Great Britain, we should only delude ourselves if we did not admit that the question is closed."

After the Brussels Convention, the German Agriculturists, deluded into the belief that bimetallism might raise the price of grain, induced the Government to appoint a Commission on the subject, and the Commission has reported that it is not possible to raise the price of silver by international agreement. After twenty-one sessions the President closed the proceedings with the single remark that *these protracted debates might be useful as showing how difficult it was to find something which would evidently be desirable if it were attainable.*

On the present status of the movement let me put in evidence M. Paul Leroy Beaulieu, in *The Forum* for December, 1895:

"To-day a fixed ratio between gold and silver, and equality in monetary function between the two metals, is an arrangement long since vanished. It seems an antiquated institution, abandoned for a quarter of a century. Any restoration becomes more difficult with the passage of time. Such is the fate of silver,—a dethroned monarch. In 1876, in 1880, in 1885, even in 1890, though far less at the later dates, there were people disposed to maintain it in its former functions, or to restore those functions when they had been only recently lost. But to-day an entire new generation of adults has arisen who never knew silver in complete possession of the functions of money.

"There is not a single European country, in a normal financial condition, that attaches the slightest importance to bimetallism. From time to time some Minister utters in Parliament a few equivocal words on the subject, seeking to avoid stripping the bimetallists absolutely of all hope. But America must not be duped by these ambiguous expressions. At bottom not a country, not a government of Europe, has the least wish to make the least change in the established monetary system, that is, in the pre-eminence of gold, and the secondary and circumscribed function of silver."

As there were proposals as early as the beginning of the seventeenth century, or really the closing of the sixteenth century, that is, three hundred years ago, for an international common ratio, we can see from the present status what progress the theory or proposition for international bimetallism has made.

Says Mr. Giffen :

" After so much bimetallic clamor as we have suffered for twenty years, sober men may be interested to see how overwhelming are the facts and the economic opinion against the bimetallist, and how little claim bimetallism has to be a competing monetary theory with gold monometallism."

Says Prof. W. A. Shaw :

" The verdict of history on the great problem of the nineteenth century—bimetallism—is clear and crushing and final, and against the evidence of history no gainsaying of theory ought for a moment to stand."

To conclude this part of my subject I will repeat :

1st. The quantitative theory — the international bimetallists' theory—lacks foundation in any known principle of economic law, and is a fallacy.

2d. That the economic phenomena of the past fifty years indicate that prices of commodities move in obedience to natural and inherent causes, independent of circulating money quantities.

3d. By natural law, there is but one way to provide for bimetallism in any country, and that is to make the more precious metal the standard, and then float such an amount of the cheaper metal as can be kept upon an undoubted equality through free interchangeability.

"FREE SILVER."

A CCORDING to the press dispatches of February 8th, Representative Hall of Missouri charged on the floor of Congress that Senators who voted for free coinage had, according to "credible information," privately said they believed free coinage would bring upon this country national and individual bankruptcy and ruin. He declared that the greatest sin of the present age was the cowardice of statesmen.

We have shown under the head of "International Bimetallism" that it has been rejected by every Western power of any importance, and it should be borne in mind that it is not claimed by any prominent advocates of that theory, for example, Lavelleye of Belgium, Cernuschi of France, Ahrendt of Germany, Walras of Switzerland, Seyd (deceased) or Gibbs or Helm of England, or Andrews or Walker of the United States, that the unrestricted free coinage of silver by any *one* government now maintaining a gold standard could be otherwise than disastrous. On the contrary, they declare in print that they do not desire to debase the standard of value; they would have every debt paid in gold or its equivalent. And this is the tone of bimetallists generally in Great Britain and Continental Europe. To all of which I repeat: *When the two money metals*

*have unlimited free coinage at fixed ratios, and are
legal tender, the cheaper will, under all possible circumstances, drive the dearer out of circulation.*

———

We now come to the present most aggravated form
of the silver money question,—its independent, unlimited free coinage by the United States. Alongside
of me in business is a man of the utmost probity, who
regards gold and silver as Siamese twins, and in effect
says, " What God hath joined together let not man put
asunder," though the commercial relations of the two
metals have been, since the dawn of history, from 1 of
silver to 1 of gold to 34 of silver to 1 of gold, and in
the past three hundred years France alone has changed
their ratios more than one hundred times to keep this
pair of celestials in double harness. Nevertheless, this
does not daunt my doughty friend, who ascribes all the
trouble to the " natural cussedness " of mankind, the
iniquitous machinations of avaricious goldbugs, and
simply relies upon the leaven of genuine Christianity
to keep the discordant couple in harmony. He finds
Love a solvent for all refractory elements in life, an
ounce of which he maintains in his philosophy on a
parity with a pound of knowledge, that is, of the
scientific methods in conformity with economic law. In
support of his doctrine he quotes :

> "While Honor's haughty champions wait
> Till all their scars are shown,
> Love walks unchallenged through the gate
> And sits beside the throne."

Recently one of our California Congressmen whom
I met, after saying he would leave in a few days for

Washington, to vote for the unlimited free coinage of silver, volunteered the opinion that there is no economic law that is an absolute criterion in finance, and that the people are bound to have the unlimited free coinage of silver.

It is very certain that the average man knows far less of finance and the laws of economic science than he does of the solar system and astronomical science; and natural law governs economic science as surely as it does the movements of the planets. Popular clamor should never be heeded in finance any more than in astronomy; for, as we have already shown under the "Natural Law of Money" and "International Bimetallism," all history proves that economic law operates with as much certainty in the one as gravitation does in the other.

Prof. Nicholson wisely observes :

"If it is once generally believed that questions of currency can be decided off-hand by popular vote, the way becomes open for great national calamities."

As indicating the views of the free silver agitators, I quote from the proceedings of a Silver Convention in Iowa :

"The demonetization of silver was a colossal conspiracy and crime, the greatest ever perpetrated against the human family. It was demoniac."

Senator Pfeffer of Kansas declared :

"It matters not of what money is made, or what its intrinsic value is. What gives value to the coins is law, nothing else. Our dollars ought to represent our property, all that we have, and not merely the little gold in our possession; and our money ought to be made of material which, in small bits, would have no appreciable market value. Then it would not be 'cornered,' and when war or hard times should come it would not slink away and hide. When the people need money, they ought to have it within easy reach."

And for himself and constituents, in furtherance of such and kindred vagaries, a free silver Governor of a free silver State said that they would, if necessary, ride in blood " even unto the horses' bridles."

Senator Stewart of Nevada, in the *Overland Monthly* for November, says :

" The combination which wickedly, dishonestly and clandestinely demonetized silver and destroyed one-half of the metallic money of the world dare not admit why they did it and for whose benefit it was done,—and that it is supported by time-servers, cringing politicians, trembling debtors, office-holders with fixed incomes, and fawning hypocrites and sycophants of every name and nature."

The Silver party, in its Convention at Washington, on Thursday, January 23d, said :

" The fall of prices has destroyed the profits of legitimate industry, injuring the producer for the benefit of the nonproducer, increasing the burden of the debtor and swelling the gains of the creditor, paralyzing the productive energies of the American people, relegating to idleness vast numbers of willing workers, sending the shadows of despair into the home of the honest toiler, and building up colossal fortunes at the money centers."

Only a few weeks ago a free silver Senator from South Carolina denounced the President of the United

States as a besotted tyrant, declaiming on the floor of the Senate to this effect:

"The derangement in our financial affairs and all this cry about sound money and maintaining the honor and credit of the United States are all part and parcel of a damnable scheme of robbery, which has for its object: first, the utter destruction of silver as a money metal; second, the increase of the public debt, the issue of bonds payable in gold; and third, the surrender to corporations of the power to issue all paper money and give them a monopoly of that function."

In a debate in the United States Senate, January 30, 1896, Senator Mitchell of Oregon said:

"We must legislate to increase the value of our export commodities (including silver) so as to enable us to meet, reduce, and, if possible, wipe out the debt which to-day makes the people of this country virtually slaves to the money-lenders of Great Britain."

Irving M. Scott says, in the *Overland Monthly* for February:

"Not only have the demonetizing acts with respect to silver reduced the world's redemption money fully fifty per cent, but they have palsied its powers of recuperation, have effected a scarcity of money, and thereby infested our country's doors with countless packs of ravenous wolves."

Such are some of the hysterical utterances of the financial rough-riders of the country as they shout their fallacious doctrines to deluded adherents. The folly of the free silver agitators in the United States is but another form of the " whip-all-creation " braggadocio once so common in this country, but none the less hurtful and deplorable because common. To all of which I have repeatedly remarked in the past, and now reiterate, that if the Government of the United States can, by legal enactment, convert a given quantity of a commodity worth only fifty cents in the world's markets into one dollar of money of permanent value, why not waive the fifty cents' worth of intrinsic value and issue fiat money at once? If law can do this, why not make gold and silver equal in value, ounce for ounce? If this can be done, why levy taxes? The doctrine is, in fact, that of the advocates of inconvertible paper; only the latter are more logical. If Government is to fix prices at all, it is, of course, cheapest and easiest to go to inconvertible paper at once. The perverted views in question have all resulted from the cheap-money delusion which has made the United States monetary system the irregular and wasteful patchwork that it is. To create more money in order to raise prices in general has been the object of one faction, while another has aimed purely and directly at raising the price of silver. What has been proposed and done, therefore, has tended to aggravate monetary evils instead of lessening them.

Senator Stewart says, " *They* dare not admit why they did it and for whose benefit it was done," namely, the omission of the silver dollar from coinage,—that which he now calls " the crime of '73." As he voted for it, I will put him in evidence. In the Senate, February, 1874, Senator Stewart, replying to a question from Senator Logan, said :

" I want the standard gold, and no paper money not redeemable in gold; no paper money the value of which is not ascertained; no paper money that will organize a gold board to speculate in it."

The " gold board " referred to was the Gold Exchange in New York, which existed during the suspension of specie payments. Subsequently Senator Logan, in discussing the same subject, stated that we could not get gold to resume specie payments with. To which Stewart replied:

" When gold is invited to a country like this, with such an industrious people as we have, with our industry and our resources, I say there will be no difficulty about getting sufficient gold."

Since those words were spoken the annual production of gold in the world has increased 120 per cent.

Senator Stewart now says:

" They (the advocates of a gold standard) know full well that, if silver had the same right of mintage with gold, *the parity between the two metals would be restored and maintained, as it was for thousands of years previous to the crime of 1873*."

I wonder if he was conscious of the irony of his own words? There never has been maintained, at any place or period, an evenly operating parity between the two metals as legal tender under free coinage at fixed ratios.

He also asks:

" Does anybody doubt that Japan, China, Mexico, and other free coinage countries, are more prosperous and happy than ever before in their history? *while every gold-standard country in the world is more miserable than at any other time for the last two hundred years?"*

I have taken at random nine callings, as follows, laborer, bricklayer, stonemason, blacksmith, driver, butcher, shoemaker, carpenter, printer, and find that at present their aggregate wages for one day in San Francisco are $29.35 gold; at four Pacific Coast commercial centers, combined average, $25.56 gold; in commercial centers east of Missouri River, $22.17 gold; in Mexico, $8.17 in silver; in China, $3.25, and in Japan, $2.19, also silver, though since the Chino-Japanese war wages are rising in China as well as Japan. McMasters quotes the same number and calling of workmen in New York as earning, in the period between 1770–1800, for one day, $7.35 in silver. Thomas Carlyle, in his "Past and Present," quaintly records that Milton received for his "Paradise Lost," and other works, £10 in installments and a narrow escape from hanging. And Bishop Latimer, in one of his sermons, shows that in his time £8 was not infrequently the yearly wage of a parish priest, which he very justly denounced as niggardly. In money of the present time it would be only about $10.

The average wage-earner in Japan or China gets no more in silver than one-eighth the rate obtained in this country in gold, and in Mexico, right alongside of us, as a rule no more in silver than one-third the rate received in this country in gold. I also refer to the labor statistics quoted under "International Bimetallism."

Senator Stewart says, "One-half the metallic money of the world has been destroyed." Mr. Scott says, "Reduced the world's redemption money 50 per cent.'

There never has been any destruction of or reduction in the amount of silver money. On the contrary, it has increased over 75 per cent in 45 years. Taking Mulhall's figures for 1860, $4,000,000,000, and 1890, $7,973,000,000, as a basis, and adding the total product, mint ratios, 1891–95 inclusive, and deducting from these five years 40 per cent for the arts, the amount of gold and silver money would now be approximately $9,100,000,000, or an increase of 134 per cent since 1860. But taking other figures, in 1860 the world's total stock of coin, estimated, was $4,000,000,000; in 1895, as per United States Mint Report, $8,157,000,000; and the present stock of metallic money exceeds $8,200,000,000, an increase of 105 per cent in 45 years. This money is divided at the present time: Gold, $4,130,000,000; silver, $4,070,-000,000.

Four thousand and seventy millions of dollars is the mint value of the silver money in the world, its commercial value being approximately sixty-five cents per ounce; and nearly half of it represents silver monometallism in Oriental lands. Does any sane man believe that unlimited free coinage by the United States of America would increase the market value of this mass of silver two thousand millions of dollars? Although eighty-five per cent of the total is full tender, it possesses, practically speaking, no more commodity value in one place than another, as compared with gold, because, in the relations between gold and silver in India, China, Japan and Mexico, silver is subject to practically the same commodity price that it would be with us. Throughout the whole history of the subject, whatever may have been the legal ratio enacted between gold and silver coins, gold and silver themselves have always had a commodity value independent of these ratios ; and this commodity value invariably controlled the purchasing power of each money under unlimited free coinage of both metals. In all large transactions of ancient or medieval times, the settlement of obligations was in either gold or silver by weight (as it is now in China), and without reference to coinage ratios, which were variable and constantly set at naught by the commercial status of the metals, that is, by the will of the people,—the supply and demand.

However, so far as the world's stock of silver is concerned, it is only when it is employed in international exchanges or in the industrial arts that it is estimated at its bullion value in gold and subjected to a discount. In all countries where it is the legal standard, as well as in countries that have a so-called " limping " standard, like the United States and the States of the Latin Union, it circulates as money at its full legal parity with gold, and to the extent of $630,000,000, which represents the subsidiary silver in circulation, is current at nearly seven per cent more than its bullion value in standard silver coins.

Of the $4,070,000,000 silver in circulation, according to the Mint Director's last report, $1,900,000,000, or nearly one-half, is held in Oriental countries, where it is the "standard of value," and hence cannot be at a discount in the domestic commerce of those countries; while over $1,720,000,000 is held by the United States, the Latin Union, Germany, Spain and Great Britain,

all of which circulates at its full parity with gold. A
no period in history has there ever been such a vast
volume of silver coin performing the functions of
money. And, as proof of this, while the world's
produce of silver since 1873, when its alleged demonetization occurred, has been $2,754,452,900, its coinage
has been $2,756,423,015. This, of course, includes
recoinage. Moreover, it has been persistently asserted
by leading bimetallists that silver has not depreciated,
and will buy as much now as it ever could. And, to
demonstrate that proposition, we have been treated to
an amount of arithmetical jugglery that might well
make Hermann, prince of prestidigitators, or even an
Indian fakir, turn green with envy.

In this connection Mr. Scott should consider the
present and past relations of the copper " cash " with
the silver taels in China.

To merely touch upon Mr. Scott's assertion regarding
what he deems reduction by reason of the gold standard,
I may say that we find, upon reference to authorities,
that the production of gold (I am now speaking of gold
and silver as commodities) was, in 1874, $91,000,000 ;
in 1876, $104,000,000 ; in 1878, $119,000,000; in 1890,
$120,000,000; in 1892, $147,000,000; in 1894, $180,000,-
000; and in 1895, breaking all previous records, it was
$200,000,000.

Silver represented, in 1870, $51,000,000; in 1874,
$70,000,000 ; in 1884, $91,000,000; in 1894, $106,-
000,000; in 1895, $110,000,000; wherefore, I repeat,
there has never been any destruction of or reduction in
the volume of silver money.

As Mr. Scott practically advises this country to abandon the gold standard and adopt the unlimited free coinage of silver, presumably at a ratio of 16 to 1, which is about twice its actual value, and which means cheap-silver monometallism,—I would ask what effect such a policy would have upon the welfare of the men whom he employs, and also upon that of the people of California whose gains and earnings are largely represented by the hundred and seventy-five millions of deposits on a gold basis in the savings and commercial banks of this State? In other words, does he, or does any one, really believe that his workmen, or anybody's workmen, or the people at large, would be benefited by being paid their wages, or their deposits in banks, on a depreciated silver basis, instead of a gold basis, as now?

In the Elizabethan reformation of the English coinage under Sir Thomas Gresham in the sixteenth century, the Queen, in her proclamation, said: "The loss in the base money falls principally on *pensioners, soldiers, hired servants, and all other poor people who live by any kind of wages,* and not by rents of land or trade or merchandise." This is in accordance with a natural law as inexorable as gravitation, that no legislation can evade or set aside.

The way in which the subject of free silver coinage is discussed by many of its advocates would, without disrespect, suggest that they expected to be able to go forth with a sack and obtain money for nothing; but there is no royal road to wealth, and all should consider the evils that would result to the industrial classes of this country from the substitution of a currency based on silver instead of gold.

Every person should candidly reflect upon the industrial condition and wage-earning opportunities of human kind in silver-standard countries as compared with the gold-standard countries. It is only in the gold-standard countries that high wages have been achieved. Every country in the world that has unrestricted free coinage is on a silver basis, and low wages prevail. There is not a gold-standard country in the world that does not use silver as auxiliary; but there is no silver-standard country that does or can use gold as auxiliary, except by specific contract or as hoarded treasure.

Why any considerable portion of the American people should have believed, or can now believe, that the unrestricted free coinage of silver could possibly be a benefit, or that silver and silver-producers should be deemed entitled to any more consideration than wheat and cotton and the men that plant and cultivate them, is simply astonishing.

Professor Andrews stands aghast at the idea of socialism,—speaking of anarchism, nihilism and socialism in the same breath as corelated,—thus:

" That labor is the sole cause of wealth, and that things are wealth exactly in proportion as they embody labor, is a fundamental tenet of socialism, anarchism and communism, the admission of which leaves one no logical defense against the general doctrine of those people."

Yet, " doing something for silver " is class socialism as pernicious in effect as that of the greenback legislation, which is probably one of the most aggravating examples known in this country of home markets that do not qualify for the farmer when his products are brought into competition in the world's markets—which fix home prices—with the products of Argentine peons, Indian ryots and Russian peasants.

The alleged popular desire for free coinage, upon which so much stress has been laid, is presumably based on a belief in the public mind that silver, given free scope, would cure or at least mitigate industrial depression, caused, as alleged, by scarcity of money; and that it would contribute largely to the relief of farm mortgage or note debtors, both of which are points upon which the advocates of free silver also place especial emphasis. An advocate of free silver has said:

" It is not a question of interest to the people whether the gold and silver bullion owners may have the right to have their metal coined into legal-tender dollars, but it is of vital interest that those who carry the burden of $2,500,000,000 of debts that are liens on their property shall have the right to the use of both metals for legal-tender money to pay those vast debts."

The question arises, Would *even they* be helped under the independent, unlimited free coinage of silver? Any one possessing silver bullion would have the same coined, because of the artificial value placed upon it by Government, and use it to his own advantage. How would farmers with mortgaged farms obtain such silver but by exchanging their commodities for it, or by executing fresh mortgages? When asked how they are to get possession of a more plentiful supply of money, if on a free silver basis it should be more plentiful, they cannot tell. That our wheat farmers have suffered extremely admits of no doubt. In addition to drought and other climatic vicissitudes, they have suffered from the competition of India, Argentina and Russia, thereby demonstrating the fallacy of the home-market delusion; and, latterly, cable and trolley cars and the bicycle have come in to lower the prices of their horses and lessen the demand for feed grains, etc. But how would a depreciated currency, such as would be produced by the unrestricted free coinage of silver, help them? In California their obligations are in terms of gold. In any event contraction and panic would be the first result of a change, because gold would be driven out of circulation. Moreover, gold has by law been the standard for twenty-three years, a period of time long enough to permit six generations of ordinary farm or land mortgages to expire by limitation, the average life of such mortgages being less than four years.

It is averred by Mr. L. M. Dembitz, of Louisville, Ky., in his monograph, " The Free Coinage Problem," that, " making all proper deductions, it will be found that among the bread-winners of the United States there is not one in a hundred who owns a heavily incumbered home farm, and who could, with any approach to a semblance of right, demand the passage of a law shaking off or lightening his burden."

Debtors might avail themselves of a free-coinage law to pay their debts in cheaper money if their creditors should not be alert enough for them; but capitalists will be equal to the situation as regards future bargains, for by universal consent commercial communities may by contract free themselves from the burdens of such an act. The gold standard was, in fact, brought into use in England 180 years ago by the community contracting in this manner, and the experience on the Pacific Coast, as well as in England and elsewhere, shows that the commercial community is everywhere ready enough to use other than an enforced money if they do not quite like it.

But there would be no protection whatsoever for the wage-earner of any kind. He would be as a lamb led to the slaughter. The shopkeeper who sells goods, and the capitalist who rents houses or lands, can raise the prices thereof by their own volition; but the workman who buys goods and rents houses or lands cannot similarly raise his own wages. Of all the contrivances for cheating the laboring classes of mankind, none is more effectual than a currency that is not convertible into metallic money of intrinsic equivalency. In this country to-day the laboring man receives a dollar equal to gold worth 100 cents, but with silver dollars of independent, unlimited free coinage he would be cheated of one-half of his dollar. Free silver coinage practically means cheating creditors out of one-half their dues. The adoption of free silver means silver monometallism, with silver coin depreciated one-half. The maintaining of both metals as money should be such that each should equal the other. That would be true bimetallism, and is only possible with gold as the standard and silver as auxiliary freely interchangeable.

It is frequently asserted by advocates of the independent, unlimited free coinage of silver by the United States Government, that the prices of commodities, particularly wheat, have steadily moved in sympathy

with the price of silver. An examination of this subject has shown that within the past twenty-three years
the fluctuations, for example, in wheat, corn and cotton,
have almost invariably occurred because of an increase
or a decrease in the world's supply; that is to say,
when the crops were light, prices increased, and, when
crops were heavy, prices decreased;—beef and pork following the fortunes of the cereals to a less degree;—and
such fluctuations show continuously throughout the
period named, to wit, twenty-three years, from 1873 to
1895 inclusive, with no indication that the changes in
prices were caused or governed by silver quotations in
any way. In other words, the general downward tendency in the price of wheat has been due mainly to the
increased product, for export, in Argentina, India,
Russia and the United States also. Let us take the
coffee crop, almost entirely confined to silver-using
countries, and of the present value of $250,000,000 per
annum. It has doubled in quantity since 1870, yet the
demand has at the same time so increased that the
price is now approximately 18 cents per pound in gold,
as against an average of less than 11 cents for five
years, from 1856 to 1860, an increase of 66 per cent.
Cotton varied 77 per cent in 1895. Wheat declined in
eighteen years — that is, from 1879 (date of gold
resumption) to 1896—45 per cent; corn 15 per cent;
oats 15 per cent; lard 3 per cent; mess pork increased 3
per cent; butchers' beef 13 per cent,—a superficial average decline on these six articles of 11 per cent; while we
have shown under "International Bimetallism" that in
the same period transportation of all kinds and manufactures generally declined over 50 per cent, which must

surely be deemed a blessing, particularly as wages increased during the same period. What the explanation is of this situation is given in Professor Marshall's " Principles of Economics : " " A rise in the efficiency of any one group of workers may tend to glut the market with their wares, but a general increase in the efficiency of all workers would increase the national dividend and raise earnings nearly in proportion." This, I think, fairly accounts for the fact that wages have in the aggregate largely increased during this century, while as a whole prices of commodities have fallen, but not nearly so much as the general outcry would indicate, as can be seen from the following table from Schoenhof's " Money and Prices : "

Variation of Prices and Approximating Totals of Index Numbers.

	1845–50.	1879.	1884.	1888.
1. Coffee	100	140	106	166
2. Sugar	100	55	54	49
3. Tea.	100	111	92	64
4. Tobacco	100	156	200	244
5. Wheat	100	75	73	58
6. Butchers' meat	100	127	123	108
7. Cotton	100	73	92	90
8. Raw silk	100	113	117	117
9. Flax and hemp.	100	80	76	66
10. Sheep's wool	100	107	98	111
11. Indigo	100	164	151	129
12. Oils.	100	104	110	74
13. Timber.	100	115	100	80
14. Tallow.	100	83	113	73
15. Leather	100	146	139	133
16. Copper.	100	72	71	91
17. Iron	100	77	69	67
18. Lead.	100	84	70	90
19. Tin	100	77	104	173
20. Cotton, Pernambuco. . .	100	71	74	70
21. Cotton yarn.	100	88	99	90
22. Cotton cloth	100	81	88	87
Totals of index numbers . .	2,200	2,202	2,221	2,230
Price of silver per ounce . .	60½d.	49½d.	51d.	44⅛d.

Thus in a period of forty years,—1845–50 to 1889,—
considering the prices of commodities, we find the following advances:

Butchers' meat.	8 per cent.
Raw silk	17 "
Indigo	29 "
Leather.	33 "
Coffee.	66 "
Tin.	73 "
Tobacco (internal revenue tax).	144 "

The cry of distress has been chiefly because of wheat
and cotton. If, during an average of eighteen years,
the fall in silver caused wheat and cotton to fall, why
did it not cause coffee, tobacco, beef, mess pork, lard,
etc., to fall? In the year 1895, as stated, cotton varied
from 5.28 to 9.38 per pound, or 77 per cent, and coffee
was higher from 1890–95 than it had been for twenty
years preceding, the average being 18 cents per pound
for the six years named. Why? Because of a steadily
increased demand for it.

Let us now consider the side of the creditor. There
are in the United States due or pending from savings
banks, building and loan associations, and life and fire
insurance companies, several thousand million dollars,
to say nothing of railroad and other corporation stocks
and bonds. There are 18,000,000 wage-workers
whose earnings, let us say at $400 each, yield them
$7,200,000,000 per annum. Think of the hardships
that through these immense interests would be pressed
upon the working people by a change to the free coinage of silver,—a 50 per cent reduction in the standard
of measure and capital valuations.

In the monetary inquiry of Great Britain in 1381, Richard Aylesbury is reported to have said:

" The agreement of the gold with the silver could not be effected unless the money were changed; but *that* he dared not propose, on account of the general damage which would ensue."

In 1830, when France, Germany, the United States, etc., were on a silver basis, a Mr. Atwood introduced a bill into Parliament to have silver—which, as compared with gold, was then at a discount of 5 per cent in England—invested with full money functions for the payment of all obligations, to which Mr. Herries, Master of the Mint, replied, conclusively, that it would mean general bankruptcy: 1st, by demand for payment of debts in gold before silver became effective; 2d, by change of capital valuations to a silver basis. Sir Robert Peel also said it would mean general bankruptcy.

If 5 per cent depreciation would approximately occasion such results in England, what would 50 per cent do in the United States?

I take the liberty of quoting from John Locke one of several quaint and simple illustrations which he gave, in answer to a proposition from Secretary Lowndes of the British Treasury to increase the denominational value of a crown, and I trust my hearers will observe how aptly it applies to the artless theories of the silver agitators. Said Mr. Locke:

" The multiplying arbitrary denominations will no more supply nor in any ways make our scarcity of coin commensurate to the need there is of it, than if the

cloth which was provided for clothing the army, falling
short, one should hope to make it commensurate to that
need there is of it by measuring it by a yard one foot
shorter than the standard, or changing the standard of
a yard, and so getting the full denominations of yards
necessary according to the present measure. For this
is all that will be done by raising our coin as is proposed. All that it amounts to is no more than this,
viz, that each piece, and consequently our whole stock
of money, should be measured and denominated by a
.penny one-fifth less than the standard.

" *The increase of denomination does or can do nothing in the case, for it is metal by its quantity and not
denomination that is the price of things and measure of
commerce; and it is the weight of metal in it, and not
the name of the pieces, that men estimate commodities by
and exchange them for.*

" If this be not so, when the necessity of our affairs
abroad, or ill-husbandry at home, has carried away half
our treasure, and a moiety of our money is gone out
of England, it is but to issue a proclamation that a
penny shall go for twopence, sixpence for a shilling,
half a crown for a crown, etc., and immediately, without
any more ado, we are as rich as before; and, when half
the remainder is gone, it is but doing the same thing
again, and raising the denomination anew, and we are
where we were, and so on."

Lord Macaulay, reciting the events of the luckless
" administration " in Ireland of King James the Second,
in 1689, says :

" The poverty of the treasury was the necessary
effect of the poverty of the country. Public prosperity
could be restored only by the restoration of private
prosperity ; and private prosperity could be restored

only by years of peace and security. James was absurd enough to imagine that there was a more speedy and efficacious remedy. He could, he conceived, at once extricate himself from his financial difficulties by the simple process of calling a farthing a shilling. The right of coining was undoubtedly a flower of the prerogative ; and, in his view, the right of coining included the right of debasing the coin. Pots, pans, knockers of doors, pieces of ordnance which had long been past use, were carried to the mint. In a short time lumps of base metal, nominally worth near a million sterling, intrinsically worth about a sixtieth part of that sum, were in circulation. A royal edict declared these pieces to be legal tender in all cases whatever. A mortgage for £1,000 was cleared off by a bag of counters made out of old kettles.''

In discussing monetary matters, Thomas Jefferson said, as all the world's statesmen have said before and since, that the question of the difference between the value of gold and silver as money was purely a commercial question. It did not depend on legislation, or the fancy and taste of men, but on commerce, which regulates the price of commodities, and that '' the whole art of government consists in the art of being honest.''

Every attempt to enforce the acceptance by a free people of a depreciated and practically fiat currency has failed eventually, even in times of war, and generally then before the close of the wars. It is unnecessary to cite more examples, though there have been striking ones, especially in France and the United States within the past 200 years, and elsewhere throughout the world in all times ; and it is Government fiat alone that is depended upon by the advocates of the independent, unlimited free coinage of silver in the United States to make it go at $1.2929 per ounce as money. Its most vociferous spokesmen assert this vehemently. That this country should be kept in a state of continual suspense and incipient panic because of a product that is probably not the equal in commercial value of turnips or carrots, certainly not of potatoes or eggs, and which, expressed in figures, constitutes much less than one per cent of the country's product, is something amazing.

The agitation of the silver question, aggravated by "Coin's Financial School," is one of those hallucinations that have occurred from time to time in this country and elsewhere, but particularly in this country for the last twenty-five years, working incalculable evil, as all monetary schemes of like nature always and everywhere have done. Mr. Harvey's arguments do not contain a single valid reason or suggestion why this country should engage in a free-silver crusade,—should depart from a sound-money basis; and, when I use the term sound money, I mean money redeemable in coin of intrinsic equivalency, or, in other words, a dollar that is worth a dollar the world over. An American gold dollar, if melted, will yield a dollar's worth of gold anywhere.

The following is the dernier resort offered by Mr. Harvey in his "Coin's Financial School" for sustaining the independent, unlimited free coinage of silver by the United States of America:

"If it is claimed we must adopt for our money the metal England selects, and can have no independent choice in the matter, let us make the test and find out if it is true. If it is true, let us attach England to the United States, and blot her name out from among the nations of the earth."

Such folly as this would seem to require no comment, but Mr. Harvey is not alone in it. Some of our public men, certainly the ablest, so far as the Eastern communities of this country are concerned, suggested proscriptive legislation against Great Britain to compel that country to co-operate with the United States in the unrestricted free coinage of silver at a ratio of 16 to 1,—the most egregious folly of the times. And what is to be thought of the action of Congress as a body in refusing to incorporate the word "gold" in the terms of bonds which were to be offered only for gold. While disavowing any sentiment of disrespect to individual believers in free silver and greenbacks,—for while opposed to heresy I can respect heretics,—I must say that in view of all the facts, which are too numerous to cite here, the action of Congress in refusing to incorporate the word "gold" was in my opinion indefensible, and it was repeated, and is only in accord with the vice inherent in the general agitation for free silver, namely, a desire to pay a creditor something less than one owes. It was an action in its essence not wholly unlike that of the North Carolina banks, about 1821, that loaned their own irredeemable notes to the public on condition that the customers' discounted paper be paid in specie. What inference should honest men draw from the noncommittal action of Congress? If a banker knew a borrowing customer to be maneuvering to pay his debts in money of less value than that borrowed, how long would the banker trust that customer ?

Talleyrand admonished the National Assembly during the French Revolution in the following significant language :

" You can arrange it so that people shall be forced to take a thousand francs in paper for a thousand francs in specie, but you never can arrange it so that the people shall be obliged to give a thousand francs in specie for a thousand francs in paper."

But did the National Assembly heed the timely suggestion ? Not one whit. In effect they said, " Vox populi, vox Dei ! " and rushed on pell mell to ruin.

The same thing has just occurred in Argentina. It had been the general boast among those who were pushing on the " boom " there that Argentina was an " exceptional country," and that the ordinary laws of trade, currency and banking, however inexorable in their operation elsewhere, had no significance or applicability in the Argentine Republic.

Referring to Senator Mitchell's declaration for raising the price of silver and other products by legislation, as another exhibition of political subserviency to supposed popular clamor, I take the liberty of mentioning two planks in the State platform of a political party, in convention assembled at Sacramento, June 20, 1894, favoring the free and unlimited coinage of silver at the ratio of 16 to 1 ; and for the protection of the farmer, declaring that " the Government of the United States should reduce the cost of transporting the staple agricultural products from American seaports to foreign seaports, to the end that the prices of the products should be advanced;" adding, "and for that purpose, inasmuch as an export can be protected in no other manner, we pronounce ourselves in favor of the use of a limited portion of the receipts of the United States customs for such purposes," etc. I only wish to show by these examples what absurdities men will commit themselves to in the pursuit of gain or political place and power. Even Mr. Harvey has not equaled in folly the two examples of local origin cited.

For thirty years these United States of America have fumbled and shilly-shallyed with the financial and fiscal problems of the country as if there were no economic laws on the subject known to civilized peoples, have treated money from the standpoint of sentiment, hysteria, popular clamor and political subserviency, and taxation from that of personal aggrandizement;—while there is no law of the universe known to man and judged by human experience that works more inexorably than certain well-known economic laws. What is the excuse offered for such folly? The same that France offered when she issued forty-five thousand million francs of assignats; that Argentina offered when ten years ago she plunged into a financial debauch in a fool's paradise of cheap money, ending in ruin, to wit, that "We are an exceptional country, and there is no absolute criterion of economic laws;" in short, that we can defy all the teachings of human experience. Whom the gods would destroy they first make mad.

It is often asked by the advocates of free silver, Why do bankers generally favor gold? The answer is: 1st, it is honest and an equivalent; 2d, experience has proven it to be the best standard of value; 3d, in the aggregate four-fifths of all they represent belongs to the masses, and in protecting themselves they protect the people. In other words, the man who pursues rational and conservative methods to avoid or to lessen the danger of financial confusion and disaster is the man who seeks to maintain the best standard, thereby protecting himself as well as his fellow-men,—those upon whose favor his prosperity depends.

If a nation that has reached the gold stage of industrial development should adopt the single silver standard, it would surely place itself under a disastrous disadvantage in its commercial transactions with gold-standard nations, which at the present time represent more than 70 per cent of the commerce of the world, and would involve itself, temporarily at least, in national and individual bankruptcy. Any attempt to make the cheaper of two metals the standard—and the free coinage of silver means no less—will, under all possible circumstances, expel the dearer from circulation.

I venture the opinion that however much unrest, perturbation and travail any Western power may go through in a monetary way, it will, if true to its best interests, be sure to adopt at last the best standard of value, that is, the one of intrinsic equivalency; and intrinsic equivalency is determined, not by statutory enactment, congresses or conferences, but by the value placed upon a given commodity by the commercial world; and by this token gold is the true standard of value. It is not a question of politics, but of science and ethics, and one of superlative importance.

To legislate that over $5,000,000,000 of savings and capital in savings and commercial banks, all the fire and life insurance obligations of the country, and all the railway and other bonds and interest due thereon,— an aggregation of say $20,000,000,000,—should be paid in silver, on an unrestricted free-coinage basis, to say nothing of seven thousand millions of dollars per annum of wages to the people at large, would be to work an injustice that could not be anything less than nationally calamitous in its results. For the United States to engage in the independent, unlimited free coinage of silver would simply be financial insanity. And while I cannot believe that, in the final appeal to the common sense and right principle of the American people, they will commit the government of this country to a policy of economic madness and repudiation, the agitation by free silver advocates and the attitude of the United States Senate have already imposed incalculable loss upon the people and now seriously retard the return of industrial activity and general prosperity.

" Money is essentially rebellious to the orders of government. It comes without being called and goes without being arrested,—is deaf to advances and insensible to threats." With unlimited free coinage it is impossible to have both metals circulate simultaneously, concurrently and indiscriminately. We must choose between them and accept one as the standard.

UNDER WHICH KING, BEZONIAN?

CURRENCY.

SENATOR SHERMAN, in his article, "Deficiency in Revenue the Cause of Financial Ills," in *The Forum* for April, in speaking of greenbacks, etc., which he has termed "A truly American currency," says:

" They are a debt of the United States without interest and without other material cost to the Government than the interest on the cost of the coin or bullion held in the Treasury to redeem them."

In considering the subject of currency it seems pertinent to define standards and measures of value.

" The giving of money for a commodity is termed buying, and the giving of a commodity for money, selling. Price, unless when the contrary is particularly mentioned, always means the value of a commodity rated in money."—McCULLOCH.

A standard of value is simply a definite quantity, by weight, of pure metal designated by law as the unit of account, usually represented by coins whose weights are multiples or divisional parts of the unit thus designated. It is not, however, necessarily a coin itself, but may be simply a theoretical unit of weight, represented by no existing coin, as is the case with the money tael of China, or an actual unit of weight, as the pound of sterling silver formerly was in England.

It is, therefore, simply an immutable unit of magnitude representing a unit of account, and is employed as a numerator by weight of standard coins representing its multiples and divisional parts, to which the law affixes certain names as a means of identification, and which indicate the denominate or numerary values of such coins, by means of which the ratio or relations of exchangeable value subsisting between standard money and commodities, or between commodities as rated in money, are expressed and determined. As exchangeable value, which is synonymous with price, is only an ideal relation subsisting between things commutable, having neither length, breadth, thickness, weight nor volume, it cannot be measured by a mere mechanical application of the standard unit of measure to the thing measured, as in the case of all other standard measures. A standard of value, therefore, unlike other standards, performs its functions as a measure of value by means of its intrinsic equivalency in exchangeable value as a commodity, as determined by its market price as compared with that of the thing to be measured, and for which it is to be exchanged. Its exchangeable value, therefore, as a commodity in the markets of the world, will always control the purchasing power of coined money regardless of its denominate value as fixed by law.

A measure of value differs from a standard of value in this, that it may consist of anything which possesses exchangeable value, whether in the form of money, commodities or services which may be given in payment as an exchangeable equivalent of the thing bought as rated in standard coins of account. When, therefore, coined money is given in payment of a commodity purchased, it performs the double function of serving both as a standard and a measure of value. But as in the latter capacity it does not represent two per cent of the exchanges arising from trade and commerce, by far its most important function is as a standard of value for rating the different signs of value employed in effecting the exchange and distribution of the products of human industry. And for such purposes its capacity is absolutely unlimited, as it is only employed as an economic potential for differentiating arbitrated exchanges in the liquidation of balances and settlement of credits, and not as a material recompense or exchangeable equivalent as when employed as a measure of value. This technical distinction is only important in so far as it serves to refute the alleged insufficiency of the supply of gold for the purposes of currency, seeing that fully 98 per cent of the exchanges it effects are simply as a standard of value in the rating and differentiation of exchanges effected by credits and other instrumentalities of trade and commerce serving as the actual measures of value, and that this alleged insufficiency has no connection with the phenomena of falling prices and the depression of trade.

Succinctly stated: A measure of value may be anything possessing exchangeable value which is actually given or exchanged for anything purchased, as its exchangeable equivalent as rated in standard money, and, therefore, always expresses the relation of value subsisting between money of account and commodities, or between commodities compared one with another.

A standard of value is simply a fixed and immutable unit of weight of a precious metal designated by law as the unit of account by which all other values are rated, by means of its own intrinsic equivalency as a commodity in the markets of the world. It is usually represented by coins, but not necessarily so. Its exchangeable value as a commodity will therefore always control the purchasing power of coined money regardless of its denominate or numerary value.

Imaginary, ideal or merely denominative money, not infrequently called money of account, bank or book money, makes its appearance in the records of Western Europe in the twelfth century, while an actual coinage to correspond therewith does not appear noted anywhere until a century later. The first of this denominative money that we read of—after the actual gold augustale of Frederick of Sicily—is the florin de sigillia, or florin of the public seal, in the banking and commercial life of Florence; the next is the zechina grossi and zechina d'or of Venice. Later we find these conventional measures of value appearing in accounts of Flanders,—Antwerp, Bruges, etc., and of Germany at Nuremburg and Hamburg, and ultimately in the pound sterling of England.

A feature of accounting by these fixed standards, beginning with their adoption in Florence and subsequently in Venice, was the integrity and general satisfaction that characterized commercial and financial transactions under them, that is to say, the fixity and approximate equivalency of payments thus assured by the adjustment of actual money to these standards in banks and commercial houses; and it appears that wherever this practice existed it drew around the nations

or the peoples so operating an ever-increasing volume
of business, though of course the general trend of trade,
from the dawn of history, has been from the East
toward the West. ·Thus the commercial importance of
Florence and Venice during the thirteenth, fourteenth
and fifteenth centuries was transferred to Flanders* in
the sixteenth century, and to London in the seventeenth,
eighteenth and nineteenth.

It may also be in order to give examples of the
difference there may be between currency, standard
money, money of account,—in terms,—and money of
redemption.

In Colonial Virginia: Warehouse receipts were the
currency, pounds, shillings and pence the money of
account, and tobacco the money of redemption.

In Colonial Massachusetts: Wampum was the currency, pounds, shillings and pence the money of account,
and beaver skins the money of redemption.

In Colonial South Carolina: Warehouse receipts the
currency, pounds, shillings and pence the money of
account, and rice the money of redemption.

In California: Gold has chiefly been the currency,
dollars and decimals the money of account, and gold of
ultimate redemption.

Throughout the United States at present, greenbacks, Treasury demand notes, National bank notes
and silver certificates are the currency, dollars and
decimals the money of account,—in terms,—and, legally,

---

*The capture of Antwerp by the Duke of Parma, one of the Generals of Philip of
Spain, in the latter part of the sixteenth century, caused the downfall of that city's
commerce, and abruptly transferred the same to London, including not less than one-
third of the merchants and manufacturers who had previously resided at Antwerp.

both gold and standard silver the money of redemption; — though it being declared in the so-called Sherman Act of July 14, 1890, to be the policy of the Government to maintain the parity of the two metals, the rule in actual practice has been to use gold only as the money of ultimate redemption, this being essential to the maintenance of silver on a parity with gold.

The term " money of account " is used very indiscriminately, ordinarily referring to sterling, as in actual commerce there are at present, strictly speaking, only two moneys properly so designated,—the English pound sterling and the Chinese tael, both of which names are merely denominative, there being no such coins as a pound or a tael. The English sovereign, however, represents the pound sterling. The Chinese tael is the oldest ideal or conventional standard of value of which we have any account, dating back some 2,000 years. The Shanghai tael represents 568 grains of pure silver, and the Hong Kong or Canton $579\frac{84}{100}$ of pure silver, which accounts for the difference in exchange on Hong Kong, Canton or Shanghai.

For this country the United States Statutes define dollars and decimals as money of account. But the variety of money actually in use is notable, there being no less than ten different kinds, namely, coppers, nickels, subsidiary silver, standard silver, silver certificates, standard gold, gold certificates, greenbacks, demand notes, and National bank notes.

However, despite all the noisy contention of the past twenty years as to the unit of value, and the standard of value, and although the Revised Statutes and Statutes at Large direct the issue and prescribe the uses, more or less limited, of several kinds of currency, as already stated, to but one do they assign the office of standard. To but one dollar—the gold dollar—do they assign the function of "a unit of value." The function of a gold dollar as the unit of value is, therefore, unqualified and unquestionable. Its value *is the unit of value*. Its measure *is made the only measure*. To that measure every other dollar must conform, while other dollars exist, and this law of Congress stands. Yet, despite this fact, for a score of years governors and senators have been declaiming as if gold were not the standard.

It may not be amiss to say a word here regarding the common confusion of ideas as to capital. Money may be capital, but capital is not generally money. Capital is the difference between total production and total consumption,—values at rest,—free from lien ; and for one large capitalist there are many small ones. Only that part of wealth is capital which is or may be used for the production of other wealth.

The United States affords to-day a very remarkable financial spectacle. The banks present an almost united front in favor of one policy, Congress of another. However they may differ on other questions, the bankers of the country believe that the time has come when the Government currency—United States notes and Treasury notes—should be retired ; while neither political party in Congress favors such a measure.

The attitude of the Senate particularly may be fairly expressed in the written words of a United States Senator to myself, as follows :

" You are not so broad in your views upon bimetallism as I would like to see you. But then I attribute this to your association with gold men, or with those who believe in reducing the volume of money so that they can better control the money commodity of the country, and thus take advantage of the necessities of others."

This indicates an utter misapprehension of the principles or natural law and commercial usage that govern the efficiency and movement of money. Despite two thousand years of woeful experience in all sorts of statutory devices, that is, kingly decrees and Government fiat, and the manifest fallacy thereof, we are yet confronted with the amazing spectacle of a majority of most potent, grave and reverend seigniors, our very noble and approved good legislators, sitting in the United States Senate chamber to conserve the welfare of this country, and not only entertaining the thought but asserting it, and by arbitrary legislative tactics seeking to impose a currency upon the country which would have for its maintenance as a standard of value, not intrinsic equivalency or commercial concurrence, but Government fiat merely, and out of which would inevitably ensue the collapse, disaster and misery which have attended the practical application of every such device since the world began, and always and everywhere in a special manner augmented the burdens of the working people,—the wage-earners of mankind.

The widespread delusion in the mind of this generation of Americans on the subject of money, namely, that Government fiat creates values, is peculiarly due to the Legal Tender Act of 1862, and the subsequent action of a Supreme Court in upholding the right of Congress to issue such money. Thus bad began, and worse remained behind; out of this—the continued existence of this fiat money (for, as said by Thomas Paine, regarding Continental currency, "Every stone in the bridge that carried us over seems to have had a claim upon our esteem")—was developed the silver craze.

The financial policy of the founders of our Government, as manifested in the proceedings and discussions attending the adoption of the Federal Constitution, and in their subsequent legislation, indicated sound views on money; and clearness of definition as to the proper measure of value characterized all their utterances, and all the monetary legislation of the country down to the time that the silver question made its appearance in our politics. Greenbacks, though not redeemable in coin, were exchangeable for Government bonds, that were payable, principal and interest, in coin; and coin practically meant gold, under the acts of 1834–37 and 1853, for that was really the money of ultimate redemption; and, although a majority of a Supreme Court of the United States finally declared the Greenback Act constitutional,—after such an interpretation had been denied,—there is no reason to doubt that it was the intention of the framers of the Constitution to withhold from Congress the power of making paper money a legal tender.

Pelatiah Webster, writing about the close of the Revolutionary War, and referring to Continental money, said :

" We have suffered more from this than from every other cause of calamity ; it has killed more men, pervaded and corrupted the choicest interests of our country more, and done more injustice, than even the arms and artifices of our enemies."

Judge Story, referring to the revolutionary and post-revolutionary legal-tender laws, and following the lines and phraseology of Judge Marshall's opinions, says:

" They entailed the most enormous evils on the country, and introduced a system of fraud, chicanery and profligacy which destroyed all private confidence and all industry and enterprise."

Robert Morris said :

" It has caused infinite private mischief, numberless frauds, and the greatest distress."

When the bill to make greenbacks a legal tender was being discussed in Congress, the Hon. Roscoe Conkling of New York said:

" But, passing from the constitutional objections to the bill, it seems to me that its moral imperfections are equally serious. It will, of course, proclaim throughout the country a saturnalia of fraud, a carnival for rogues. But surmounting every legal impediment and every dictate of conscience involved, viewing it as a mere pecuniary expedient, it seems too precarious and uncompromising to deserve the slightest confidence. I do not believe that you can legislate up the value of anything any more than I believe you can make generals heroes by legislation. The Continental Congress tried legislating values up by resort to penalties, but the inexorable laws of trade, as independent as the law of gravitation, kept them down. I do believe that you can legislate a value down, and that you can do it by attempting to legislate it up."

Senator William Pitt Fessenden of Maine, afterward Secretary of the Treasury, said :

" To make the best of the matter it is bad faith, and encourages bad morality both in public and in private. Going to the extent that it does, to say that notes thus issued shall be receivable in payment of all private obligations, however contracted, is in its very essence a wrong; for it compels one man to take from his neighbor, in payment of a debt, that which he would not otherwise receive, or be obliged to receive, and what is probably not full payment.

" Again: It encourages bad morals, because, if the currency falls (as it is supposed it must, else why defend it by a legal enactment), what is the result ? It is, that every man who desires to pay off his debts at a discount, no matter what the circumstances are, is able to avail himself of it against the will of his neighbor, who honestly contracted to receive something better ; I say, therefore, that another objection has been stated, of which the force must be admitted, and that is that it is bad faith.

" Again : Necessarily as a resort, in my judgment, it must inflict a stain upon national honor. We owe debts abroad yet. Money has been loaned to this country, and to the people of this country, in good faith. Stocks of our private corporations, stocks of our States and our cities, are held and owned abroad. We declare that for the interest on all this debt, and the principal if due, these notes, made a legal tender by Act of Congress, at whatever discount they shall stand, shall be receivable. Payment must be enforced, if at all, in the courts of this country, and the courts of this country are bound to recognize the law that we pass.

"Again: It necessarily changes the values of property. What is the result? Inflation, subsequent depression, all the evils which follow from an inflated currency. They cannot be avoided; they are inevitable; the consequence is admitted.

"Again: A stronger objection than all that I have to this proposition—I am stating the objections which everybody must entertain, because I suppose these facts are palpable—is that the loss is to fall most heavily upon the poor. I believe it never was disputed—it cannot be in the light of experience—that those who are injured most by an inflated currency are the laboring people, the poor. The large capitalists can bear it; but there are small capitalists in this country whom it will vastly injure. When you speak of a capitalist, in the common acceptation of the term, you mean a rich man; but every man who is free from debt and earning something, and earning a surplus, is a capitalist, and the greater number of capitalists together make up a great whole; and these are the men who suffer by the disorder of affairs,—the poor laborer, in the first place, more than all; the small capitalist, if I must so call him, next; and the rich capitalist last of all. *Such is the necessary result and consequence always of this system.*"

AND ALL THE EVILS PREDICTED CAME TO PASS.

Prof. Andrew D. White says, in his sketch of the paper-money inflation in France:

"A curious parallel may perhaps be drawn between Necker, the Finance Minister at the beginning of the

French Revolution, and the Secretary of the Treasury at the beginning of the recent struggle in our own country. Each had shown his ability to build up a fortune for himself before he entered public life; each had shown great financial skill and integrity; each had thus secured the confidence of the thoughtful part of the nation in the time of national difficulty; each had proposed measures and carried them out which resulted in great good; each attempted to stop the nation on the downward path of inflation; each was at last obliged to succumb; and each retired from the country which he had endeavored to save,—Necker to Switzerland, Hugh McCullough to England."

To the credit of Salmon P. Chase, he, as Chief Justice of the Supreme Court of the United States, said of his own creation, the greenback, in the Hepburn case, 1869:

" That the making of notes or bills of credit a legal tender for pre-existing debts is not a means appropriate, plainly adapted, or really calculated to carry into effect any expressed power vested in Congress, is inconsistent with the spirit of the Constitution, and is prohibited by the Constitution;" and, finally, " the legal-tender quality was only valuable for purposes of dishonesty. Every honest purpose was answered as well or better without it."

In 1861 the Government had none other than coined legal-tender money of intrinsic equivalency. Since Jackson destroyed "the bank" and made its revival "an obsolete idea," there had been no other. In green-backs, Congress authorized the emission, for the first time in the history of the Government under the present

Constitution, of United States paper notes as legal tender in payment of all private debts, which legal-tender clause the Supreme Court, as already stated, declared unconstitutional (as to antecedent debts), and then (on reargument before a court with two new judges) reversed that decision. Then Congress, by a ten per cent tax, swept all State bank issues out of existence to make room for National bank notes. For eighteen years those greenbacks and bank notes were inconvertible into coin; and, as I have shown in my article on " International Bimetallism," robbed wage-earners of half their earnings. As the best experts estimate,—for example, Professor Adams and Edward Atkinson,—they doubled the cost of the Civil War, and have been a continual burden ever since.

In 1875 the promise was held out of paying and extinguishing in 1879 the greenback debt. It was not done; but, on the contrary, the law of 1878 made it unlawful to cancel or retire any more greenbacks, and, even after payment, the Treasury was commanded to reissue them, pay them out again, and keep them in circulation. The law of 1878 reads thus:

" And when any of said notes may be redeemed or be received into the Treasury, under any law, from any source whatever, and shall belong to the United States, they shall not be redeemed, canceled or destroyed, but they shall be issued and paid out again and kept in circulation."

In like manner the Sherman Law of 1890 required the redeemed greenbacks to be reissued. That " endless chain " of redemption is the cause of our recent currency and gold trouble and deficiency in the amount of our gold reserve.

Congress began, in 1878, the Treasury purchasing and coining of silver dollars, and enlarged the operations in 1890, by which some 425,000,000 of silver dollars were coined. These silver dollars, manufactured by the Treasury Department, cost on an average seventy-one cents each. To-day they can be made for fifty-three cents. They were sold or paid out of the Treasury for a dollar each. Besides some $80,000,000 of subsidiary silver coins, there had been issued, under the so-called Sherman Act, $155,000,000 of new greenback debts in payment for the purchase of silver.

At the Brussels Conference of 1892 Senator Allison, one of the United States delegates, said:

" Our country, in its currency and in all its money, rests upon the gold standard. Our statutes declare that it is the settled purpose and policy of the United States to maintain silver and gold in circulation at par with each other, and there is no currency in circulation in the United States, whether it be paper or silver, that is not convertible into gold at the will of the holder."

And this is practically so, as I shall proceed to demonstrate.

The law having authorized private owners of the silver dollars to deposit them in the Treasury and receive therefor certificates payable on demand in silver dollars, some $330,000,000 of those certificates are outstanding, and, though technically redeemable in silver dollars only, are in reality an incubus on the gold reserve of the Treasury.

Until the question of the diminution of the $100,-000,000 gold reserve in the Treasury came to be publicly discussed, silver certificates were used directly in procuring gold from the Government Sub-Treasuries. The necessity to use all legal methods to keep the reserve intact stopped the practice, but silver certificates can now be used to procure gold by exchanging them through the medium of brokers, using them as bankable funds, or directly in the purchase of greenbacks or the gold itself, or by exchanging the silver dollars received for them for greenbacks. They can be deposited at par with banks, where they are accepted as bankable funds. Checks against these deposits are accepted by money brokers in payment for gold, and the commission thereon. This commission ranges all the way from $1.25 to $10 per thousand, according to the pressure. The effect which these transactions have on the reserve fund in the Treasury is that legal tenders still circulating among the people are accumulated at financial centers and presented to the Government for redemption in gold. The payments of duties in 1894 were made with silver certificates alone to the extent of 66 per cent, and 96 per cent were paid in 1895 in silver certificates and other paper currency, only 4 per cent in gold. Here we have the Gresham Law in operation on circulating notes and silver certificates.

A notable paper-money example of this kind, fifty years ago,—though the law is always in operation on any depreciated currency, metallic or paper,—was that of the so-called Suffolk Bank system of Massachusetts, viz, the circulation among the people in and about Boston of country bank notes that were at a discount; while those of the Suffolk Bank, which were at par, were *hoarded by individuals or deposited in bank*. By reason of this the circulation in Boston was at one time $24 in country bank notes to $1 in those of the Boston banks.

The sorting and culling, as we call it, or garbling, as the English call it, of currency by money brokers is a business of this kind in great cities, domestic as well as foreign, at the present time; and this is what a free silver friend calls a proof of the *"natural cussedness"* or total depravity of human nature. Whether it evidences depravity or not, it is according to human nature and that economic principle which in its wider application constitutes the Gresham Law.

There are now over $500,000,000 of paper dollars piled upon $500,000,000 more of greenbacks and Treasury demand notes, to be perpetually redeemed in gold on demand, and then reissued, to be again redeemed. This has been called, with unconscious irony, a "truly American currency." The author omitted to say that the "truly American currency" has been the arch enemy of our finances; that it occasioned, in 1893, one of the most disastrous panics known in our annals, which occurred because of the general belief that the Treasury could not long continue to redeem in gold on demand the outstanding $500,000,000 of greenbacks and Treasury notes, with the incubus of $330,000,000 of silver certificates and $200,000,000 of National bank notes on top of them. Hence the repeal of the silver-purchasing law of 1890.

This "truly American currency" has, annually, during the last few years, cost the Government $80,000,000 to get the gold for its "endless chain" of redemption, to say nothing of $175,000,000 loss on the silver, uselessly hoarded in the Government Treasury vaults, that caused it. For years past the bulk of the gold exported from this country has been for account of brokers, demonstrating that, under the practical operation of this "truly American currency," resting on a peremptory law of 1878, the United States Treasury Department is compelled to be the purveyor of gold for foreign governments, home speculators and importers of luxuries. These evils have been repeatedly pointed out by the President and Secretary of the Treasury, but Congress has failed to remedy them. The deficit in current revenues is unimportant compared with the evils growing out of the status of greenbacks.

It has been frequently alleged that bond sales for gold have been caused by the Wilson tariff and Cleveland administration, which is not so. During the four years, March 4, 1885, to March 4, 1889, Mr. Cleveland's first term, but $9,000,000 of gold was exported, under a tariff not appreciably higher than the present so-called Wilson tariff, while during the similar period from March 4, 1889, to March 4, 1893, Mr. Harrison's term, chiefly under the McKinley tariff, $213,000,000 was exported. In the three years from March 4, 1893, to March 4, 1896, over $200,000,000 was exported. The reason for these increased exports of gold—greater demand for it—is to be found in the increase of the currency, silver certificates and Treasury demand notes, set forth in Secretary Foster's report of December 7, 1892, to President Harrison, as follows:

" If $100,000,000 in gold was a suitable or necessary reserve in 1882 and 1885, it would seem clear that a greater reserve is necessary now. It should be remembered that since 1882 we have added to our silver circulation $259,016,182 in standard silver dollars coined under the old Silver Act of 1878. These dollars are nearly all outstanding, largely represented by silver certificates. We have also increased the legal-tender circulation by issuing about $120,000,000 of the Treasury notes authorized by the act of July 14, 1890, and to this we are adding about $4,000,000 each month in payment of silver bullion purchased."

When President Harrison left office the gold balance was but $113,000,000 and steadily falling. *The first year after the Sherman Act, July 14, 1890, nearly $80,-000,000 gold was exported, and during its existence more dollars of gold were exported than were acquired of silver, to say nothing of loss on silver purchased.* Why? Because of the doubt in investors' minds of our financial policy,—a redundancy of silver, silver having fallen 52 cents per ounce in three years, that is, from 119 to 67 cents.

Eighteen years ago we accumulated one hundred millions of gold to guarantee redemption of less than three hundred and fifty millions of greenbacks. This was the proportion which prudent financiers judged to be necessary. The redemption fund was about 30 per cent of the paper to be redeemed. We went on from that day adding to our stock of fiat money, partly silver dollars, partly Treasury notes, till we have placed six hundred millions on top of the original three hundred and odd millions, and now have, of all kinds of paper, over one thousand millions imposed on a diminished gold reserve, the redemption fund having at one time been as low as 12 per cent of the currency to be redeemed. The peculiar inflation mentioned by Secretary Foster now alone exceeds $400,000,000.

The two bond issues of 1894, amounting to $100,-000,000 in 10-year 5 per cents, and the third issue in February, 1895, of $62,315,400 of 30-year 4 per cents, and the fourth of $100,000,000 in February, 1896, of 30-year 4 per cents, have imposed upon the people of this country a debt of $262,000,000. That is what we must pay *directly* for Government redemption of currency; what we pay for greenbacks and Treasury demand notes that do not bear interest; what we pay for a "truly American currency;" what we pay for having the Government furnish plenty of money. As Emerson says, "We pay a price for everything we get;" or, as Forssell of Sweden said of bimetallism, "How much liquid will it take to fill a hogshead of which there is no possibility of stopping the bunghole?"

Since this paper was typed, a friend has called my attention to a series of articles in the *Ladies' Home Journal*, "This Country of Ours," by ex-President Harrison, in the August number of which he says:

"If the revenues are largely in excess of expenditures, the surplus is taken out of use in commerce and locked up in the Treasury vaults, and the money market is tightened. If the surplus is used to buy Government bonds not yet due, the market is eased. The gold reserve, too, as it is diminished by exportations of gold, or increased by bond sales, powerfully affects every business interest. What is the Treasury going to do is the query heard in every bank and counting room and store. It is unfortunate, I think, that this should be so; and the mending of existing conditions will be a task for the wisest and strongest statesmanship.

" But while the Secretary of the Treasury has a large discretion in a few directions, and may by its exercise largely influence the money market, he is, in the main, conducting a great bank on undeviating and unelastic rules, and with Congress for his board of directors. He is not chosen by the board, and is rather often than not out of harmony with it. The managers of the Bank of England may, by some small allowances in the way of interest or exchange, draw gold to its vaults from New York, and the transaction be confidential; but, if fifty dollars would suffice to hold fifty millions of dollars in the United States Treasury, the Secretary could not expend that small sum. He must stand by until the gold is gone, and then sell bonds to bring it back."

In an admirable paper read before the Reform Club of New York, Mr. W. Dodsworth of the New York *Journal of Commerce* said, in part:

" The greenback bug is the most insidious pest of these trying times. He insists upon compelling the Government to borrow 100 millions a year to save its notes from protest. He will have no interference with the distrust that is causing foreign holders of our securities to send them home in exchange for our gold.

He insists upon the acceptance of the notes being kept perpetually compulsory. By retaining this legal-tender quality, he would expose every form of investment, not expressly payable in gold, to being sooner or later liquidated in depreciated paper. He thus saps the very foundations of all credit.

"There is no hope for any reconstruction of our currency worth the trouble of getting it, unless its first step be the extinction of the legal-tender notes. So long as they remain a lawful money of redemption, there can be no fixed safety in bank paper made redeemable in them. The vitiation of the major currency must necessarily carry the vitiation of the minor. Within the last five years the greenback has suffered a deterioration of credit from which it can never recover. At home and abroad it has been discovered how easily it may become an instrument for draining off our stock of gold and transferring it to the retentive custody of the European banks. By demonstrating how easily the notes may be used for the most dangerous ends, a direct blow is struck at the credit of the Government, and, therefore, at these obligations. At last a point has been reached in the checkered history of this currency at which it hopelessly discredits itself by the exposure of its inherent lack of protection. It has become an expulsive force as against gold; and, as such, it is destructive of the only resource for its own redemption. We have long been boastfully assured that the notes were safe because the Government, with its vast resources, stood behind them. The world now discovers that this paper insidiously saps and exhausts the funds through which alone the Treasury can protect it, and thus the whole theory of State guaranty is exploded. Thus the greenback has lost its character, and it can never recover it. The great mass of public and private credit built upon it stands imperiled, and the vast interests thus threatened can never regain confidence until gold takes the place of these discredited promises to pay."

The issue of legal-tender paper was in direct violation of that principle on which so much stress was laid by our political forefathers, that no power which can be conveniently exercised by a community should be delegated to the General Government. Banking is especially that quality. Practically all our monetary enactments since the issuance of greenbacks in 1862, thirty-four years ago, have been in conflict with this principle. The Legal Tender Act, and the act taxing State bank notes out of existence,—a fine, nothing else, because there is not and never has been any increment derived from them, also the act by which silver was mechanically injected into the currency,—were such; and the effect of these several enactments in respect to money issues has been to accomplish a centralization in conflict with the principles of popular government, and to instill into the public mind utterly false conceptions of the functions and powers of government.

Since 1873, the date of the omission of the silver dollar from coinage, the politicians of this country seem to have been possessed by the idea that all the laws of political economy and finance that have been discovered by the human race in its slow and toilsome march can be violated or set aside by the United States of America; and for this economic heresy we are punished year by year, and will be punished until we learn to adopt a policy based upon well-known principles of finance and political economy. So long as forced-loan money—greenbacks—continues, and purchased silver bullion to the amount of hundreds of millions of dollars remains uselessly hoarded, our monetary system will be disturbed, and we shall suffer recurrences of panic. There never can be safety until this forced legal-tender money is canceled by payment and retirement.

The issuance of paper money is properly a function of banking, not of Government. To have it of high efficiency two conditions are absolutely essential. It must rest upon the one true basis, namely, true standard money of precious metal, and it must be bank and not Government paper. On a true standard of value, one of intrinsic equivalency, there will be no undue expansion of currency redeemable in the standard money, the same being properly fortified by reasonable security in the way of collaterals. True standard money has been well defined by Henry Cernuschi, the Italian bimetallist:

" The coins which, being melted down, retain the entire value for which they were legal tender before being melted down, are good money. Those which do not retain it are not good money."

Walter Bagehot, in " Lombard Street," says:

" In what form the best paper currency can be supplied to a country is a question of economical theory with which I do not meddle here. I am only narrating unquestionable history, not dealing with an argument where every step is disputed. And part of this certain history is that the best way to diffuse banking is to allow the banker to issue bank notes of small amount that can supersede the metal currency. As yet, historically, it is the only introduction; no nation as yet has arrived at a great system of deposit banking without going first through the preliminary stage of note issue, and of such note issues the quickest and most efficient in this way is one made by individuals resident in the district, and conversant with it."

The Government of the United States should not issue paper money. It is not properly a Government function; for the Government has no way to protect itself in the gold redemption of such notes, either in the rate of exchange or of interest or discount. Under the present status, redemption is a cause of continual expense, and this expense, in the final analysis, is borne by the people. Prof. H. C. Adams estimates the cost of the greenbacks to the people at $870,-000,000, Edward Atkinson at $2,000,000,000. See the latter's pamphlet on "Cost of Bad Money."

This country will be in financial unrest, uncertainty and apprehension until the law-making power retires the greenbacks and definitely affirms that all obligations in terms of United States of America dollars shall always and everywhere mean payment on a basis of value, of intrinsic equivalency,—in gold,—as the British pound sterling has meant for one hundred and eighty years. What is imperatively needed is not more money, but a policy of monetary legislation in conformity with the laws of finance which all human experience has shown to be certain in their action.

Our National bank system, so far as note circulation is concerned, seems to be a failure. It was inaugurated in 1866; the maximum circulation, $345,000,000, was reached in 1881; a minimum, $123,000,000, in 1890; shrinkage in nine years, 64 per cent; circulation in 1896, $200,000,000; present shrinkage from maximum, 43 per cent.

I do not propose to offer for consideration any plan for reorganizing the currency and banking system of this country, though it certainly should be organized upon an independent basis; and in the cases of Canada and Scotland we have examples of the highest monetary efficiency, with a flexible maximum of bank notes issued on a minimum of gold reserve,—15 per cent,— the notes fortified by bonds and redeemable in gold. The Canadian system is similar to that of the New York Safety Fund Bank system, which was in successful operation for nearly fifty years before the adoption of the National bank system; or the Massachusetts Suffolk Bank system, which embraced at one time 500 banks.

In the great crash of 1837, and general suspension of specie payments of 119 Massachusetts banks, with $9,400,000 note circulation, under the Suffolk system only eleven failed to resume specie payment, entailing a loss on note-holders of but $240,000, or 2½ per cent, and at that time note-holders did not have a first lien on assets. The Suffolk Bank system was an excellent one, and thoroughly stood the test of time.

The "Canadian Bank Act" of 1890 covers forty pages of printed matter. (Our own National Bank Act and amendments cover ninety-four pages.) The old Safety Fund system of New York was adopted in Canada in 1890, in order to secure the prompt redemption of the notes of failed banks, i. e., to avoid a discount on the notes of such banks pending their liquidation. Under the Canadian system the circulating notes are the first lien on the assets, and it is believed that the assets will always suffice to redeem the notes; but the delay in converting them into cash,

prior to the establishment of the Safety Fund, had led
to a temporary discount on such notes. There is now
in the Canadian "Bank Circulation Redemption Fund"
$1,800,000, and it is deemed sufficient to meet all con-
tingencies of this kind. Under the Canadian law the
Government is not responsible for the notes of failed
banks, but such notes draw interest at 6 per cent.
The maximum amount of the fund is 5 per cent of
the outstanding circulation of all the Canadian banks,
and it must be kept up to this maximum, the Minister
of Finance having power to call on the banks for additional contributions, when necessary, not exceeding 1
per cent in any year. When the assets of failed banks
are paid in, however, refunds may be made to the con-
tributing banks of the excess over 5 per cent. The
Canadian system embraces 40 banks, with 460 branches.

Regarding the Scotch banking system: Without
going into details or referring to the various acts from
the time of Queen Anne down to, say, the beginning
of the eighteenth century, it is sufficient to mention
that banking companies, with numerous partners, have
existed for a long period in Scotland. The Bank of
Scotland was established in 1695, the Royal Bank of
Scotland in 1727, and the British Linen Company in
1746. What is in general called the Scotch system
may be said to have been inaugurated about 1770, or
125 years ago.

In 1845 an act was passed relating to the Scotch
banks, by which the circulation of those then issuing
notes was confined to the average output of each for
the year preceding the 1st of May, 1845, plus an

amount equal in any one month to the average amount of gold and silver coin held during the previous month, as shown by the weekly returns,—silver to be not more than one-fourth of the gold,—which rule holds throughout Great Britain. These banks may issue notes from one pound upward, and in their returns have to distinguish the amount of notes issued of five pounds and upward from those issued below five pounds. If the monthly average circulation be above the limit of notes and coin authorized, the bank is liable to forfeit a sum equal to such excess.

At present there are but eleven banks of issue in Scotland, but these have numerous branches, extending to almost every village and hamlet, say 1,000 places. Their notes are not redeemable except at the parent banks. The issue of notes by the parent banks not secured by coin is, in round figures, fifteen millions of dollars, and the average of gold and silver coin will probably approximate thirty-five millions of dollars. Bank of England notes circulate freely, but are not a legal tender there.

There have been only three bank failures in Scotland of any importance in 125 years,—those of the Ayr Bank in 1772, the Western Bank in 1857, and the City of Glasgow Bank in 1878.

Any one of the foregoing successfully demonstrated systems, or the Baltimore or Carlisle plans recently recommended, is worthy of serious consideration and adoption by our people. The Baltimore plan dispenses with bond security for bank notes, and substitutes therefor a guaranty fund equal to 5 per cent of all bank notes outstanding, on the same general plan as the New York Safety Fund and the Canadian " Bank Circulation Redemption Fund." It restricts note issues to 50 per cent of a bank's capital, except in emergencies, when they may be increased to 75 per cent, and the Government remains responsible, as now, for the notes, and redeems them as now, having the guaranty fund and also a first lien on the assets of failed banks and on the shareholders' liability, together with the 5 per cent redemption fund required by the existing law, and the power to tax all circulating notes at the rate of one-half per cent per annum.

Even a State bank system might be preferable to the present system, because there is no reason why the admitted evils of the old banking system could not be effectively obviated, and such proper safeguards established as would be required for the protection of the people. For instance, by uniformity in the banking laws of the several States, and the issue of all notes redeemable in gold, the note-holder being secured by proper bond deposits, either State or National. Another way would be to provide, without bonds, for the issue of a certain percentage of notes, so redeemable as compared with the paid-up capital of the bank, the notes being a first lien upon the bank's assets and stockholders' liabilty in case of failure. There would be no greater danger of the revival of wild-cat banks than there is of losses under the present patchwork system.

A most important fact, that ought never to be forgotten, is that the banking facilities in existence in the

United States amount to some five thousand three hundred millions of dollars in paid-up capital, surplus and deposits, while the Government currency of all kinds at present in existence is, say, $830,000,000,—greenbacks, demand notes, silver certificates, etc. The National banks have out only $200,000,000, secured by bonds on a capital of $660,000,000. The security afforded note-holders in banking operations covers but a fraction of the risk to the depositors, the proportion of capital employed as compared to the circulating notes being approximately as 6 to 1. A National bank of $100,000 capital may fail with a million and a half of deposits, and for this amount there is no guaranty beyond the supposed solvency of the stockholders after the moiety of interest in the way of bank notes shall have been provided for. The great danger lies in the excessive creation of banking credits which the Government does not provide for, and upon which the law places no effective limitations. The writer personally knows of a failed National bank, with less than $50,000 outstanding notes to redeem, losing $90,000 by discounting drafts for one customer.

In conclusion I repeat, that what is imperatively needed is not more money, but a policy of monetary legislation in conformity with economic laws that all human experience has shown to be certain in their action. To quote Mr. Brough:

" The question is not one of politics. It is one of science and ethics, and of the first magnitude. A State wields no power so effective to lift or lower the morals of a people as its monetary legislation."

" Westward the course of empire takes its way." In the thirteenth, fourteenth and fifteenth centuries, Italy (Venice and Florence) was the center of exchanges for the commerce of Western Europe; in the sixteenth, Flanders (Antwerp and Bruges) was that center; and in the seventeenth, eighteenth and nineteenth, England gradually became the center of exchanges for the world. But in each case it grew out of standards of value, real or ideal, of intrinsic equivalency. If the United States of America be true to the teachings of history, to common sense and right, it may gain that financial supremacy in the twentieth century; but, if so, it will have to be through the gold standard and a reliable system of banking.

THE SILVER QUESTION AND HARD TIMES.

THE following articles, published in the San Francisco *News Letter* over the signature "A Layman," were occasioned by a series of papers in the *Overland Monthly* under the caption of "Hard Times," and other contributions to that periodical upon the subject of silver.

[*From News Letter, February 29, 1896.*]

Editor News Letter :

SIR : Referring to an article in the *Overland Monthly* for the present month of February by Irving M. Scott, on "Hard Times," I turn to the subject to point out inaccuracies of assertions made by Mr. Scott, in the hope that, if he again essays to advise the people what to do, he will be more careful about his statistics. The following occurs in his article :

"In 1889 the silver mines of the United States yielded $64,800,000, equal to two-thirds of the silver yield of the balance of the world. In 1894, owing to the great depreciation in the price of silver, many of our silver mines were compelled to stop work, and our yield of silver was, as measured in gold, $14,350,000. The indications are that the silver yield of our mines this year will not exceed $4,000,000. Not only have the demonetizing acts with respect to silver reduced the world's redemption money fully 50 per cent, *but they have palsied its powers of recuperation, have effected a scarcity of money, and thereby infested our country's doors with countless packs of ravenous wolves.*"

If Mr. Scott had referred to current statistical authority,—abstracts, atlases, government bureau reports, or even newspaper almanacs,—he could have materially lessened the surprising inaccuracy of these statements. He says the yield of silver as measured in gold was, for 1894, $14,350,000. As a matter of fact it was, measured in gold (commodity value), in round figures approximately $32,000,000 ; in 1895, $36,000,000. He states that the indications are that the yield of silver this year will not exceed $4,000,000. In contradiction I beg to offer the assurance that the indications are that the product of silver in the United States for this year of 1896 will approximate $40,000,000, commodity value.

Mr. Scott takes the year of 1889 as a criterion, which I accept, and will mention that the total product of the Pacific Coast and Rocky Mountain States and Territories, gold, silver, copper and lead, all of which are in the aggregate intimately related in their production throughout that section, and the falling off in commercial value was only 8 per cent in 1895 as compared with 1889, the gold product of the same localities for 1895, as compared with 1889, showing an increase of over 50 per cent. If we take our sister republic of Mexico into account, we find that the total product there of 1889 was $42,000,000, gold and silver combined, mintage ratios ; and for 1895 it was $59,000,000, an increase in the six years of 42 per cent. The production of gold alone in the world during 1895 was very considerably more than the combined product of gold and silver thirty years ago.

To go into the question of the world's product, as
Mr. Scott applies his argument to the world in setting
forth what he deems the evils of the gold standard, I
have to say that we find, upon reference to authorities,
that the production of gold (I am again speaking of
gold and silver as commodities) was, in 1874, $91,000,-
000; in 1876, $104,000,000; in 1878, $119,000,000; in
1890, $120,000,000; in 1892, $147,000,000; in 1894,
$180,000,000; and, in 1895, $200,000,000, breaking all
previous records. Silver represented, in 1870, $51,000,-
000; in 1874, $70,000,000; in 1884, $91,000,000; in
1894, $106,000,000; in 1895, $110,000,000. The price
of silver in 1889–90 was artificial, arising from the then
confident fallacy in the United States of Government
power to create values by legislative enactment.

By reference to pages 40 and 41 of the Report for
1895 of the Director of the United States Mint, Mr.
Scott will find that, of the $4,070,000,000 of silver
money in the world, $3,440,000,000, or 85 per cent,
is full tender, and that 60 per cent of that is in
Oriental lands. But the status does not confer upon
silver there any greater commodity value than in the
United States, and never did. Always and everywhere,
from the dawn of history, alongside of any legal ratio
whatever there is a commodity ratio that fixes the real
value of the metals.

In one of our city dailies of Monday, the 24th, a
prominent divine, commenting upon the moral status
of San Francisco and California, indulged in extremely
severe reflections, and, if Mr. Scott's assertion regarding countless packs of ravenous wolves infesting our

country's doors is accurate, not only the condition of San Francisco and California but the entire country is certainly very deplorable. He may well cry with Hamlet:

> " The time is out of joint. Oh, cursed spite,
> That ever I was born to set it right ! "

However, I am not disposed to take so pessimistic a view of the situation.

Mr. Scott opens and closes his article with the following quotation from Virgil:

> "To the shades you go a down-hill, easy way ;
> But to return, and rejoin the day,
> That is a work, a labor."

Something like this would be more pertinent: " How difficult it is to get back to the path of truth after floundering in the slough of error."

The hard times, which we all deplore and which Mr. Scott pathetically bewails, are largely the results of pernicious economic methods in commerce and finance, namely, of the delusion that the Government can create value by statutory enactment, and make the people rich by taxation. Honesty, patience, hard work and frugal economy are the only remedies for the ills we have largely drawn upon our own shoulders, and which we must bear until relieved by common-sense methods of our own devising. As Emerson says, " We pay a price for everything we get."

[From News Letter, March 7, 1896.]

Editor News Letter :

SIR : Recurring to Mr. Scott's article, " Hard Times," in the February *Overland*, he takes, for example, the year 1889 as a criterion, which, *with corrections*, I am willing to accept. He states the silver output of the world for that year at $64,800,000, which is approximately correct, seeing that the Director of the Mint gives it at $64,646,000. But note the method of the comparison that follows. He tells us that "in 1894, owing to the great depreciation in the price of silver, many of our silver mines were compelled to stop work, and our yield of silver was, as measured in gold, $14,350,000." Here is an apparent falling off, within the five years embraced, of $50,450,000, or 73 per cent, which is scarcely less remarkable, as a simple statement of fact, than his estimate for the current year, which he places at $4,000,000, though, as I have already stated, we have indications, from the output of 1895, that it will probably be $40,000,000.

The defect of this comparison arises from the fact that Mr. Scott states the output of silver in 1889 at its "coining" value of $1.2929 per fine ounce, while he states that of 1894 at its "commercial" value, which averaged for that year less than 64 cents per ounce. And, even at that, he states the amount inaccurately. As given above, he makes it $14,350,000, whereas the Director of the Mint gives it at $31,422,000, or something over $17,000,000 more. But the true measure of the quantity produced is its weight in ounces of pure silver and not its value. In order to show, therefore, the relative output, and the extent to which the alleged " great depreciation " of silver compelled " our miners to stop work," I give below the actual amounts as stated by the Mint Director :

1889...Fine ozs., 50,000,000	Com. value, $46,750,000	Coining value, $64,646,000
1894...Fine ozs., 49,500,000	Com. value, $31,422,000	Coining value, $64,000,000

It will thus be seen that the falling off was only 500,000 ounces, or 1 per cent of the mass, while the increase of gold was over 20 per cent, and for 1895 was 50 per cent. The same erroneous form of statements is observable in other items. He tells us, for example, that from 1873 to 1892 the world produced $2,224,000,000 of silver, estimated at $1.29 per ounce, but that " demonetization " had " reduced " this value, " as measured in gold, 50 per cent, and had reduced the world's entire amount of silver extant nearly $2,000,000,000." Now the table from which Mr. Scott apparently takes these figures shows that the " coining " value of the silver produced from 1873 to 1892 was $2,322,339,700, while its value, " as measured in gold," was $1,916,402,800, being equivalent to a discount of $405,936,900, or 17½ per cent, instead of 50 per cent, making a difference of something over $755,-000,000.

The same inaccuracy is apparent in his methods of stating the facts concerning the output of gold. " Let us not forget," he says, " that the yield of gold in California in 1851 was $81,000,000, and in the Colony of Victoria, Australia, in 1853 was $62,000,000, and that these countries are now yielding each only $13,000,000. Mr. Scott, of course, knows that in 1851 California practically represented the whole of the United States as to its gold output, as in 1853 the Colony of Victoria did the whole of Australasia. Now in 1894, according to the Director of the Mint, the United States produced $39,500,000 and Australasia $41,760,000, being in each case over three times the amount stated by him. And the world's present product far exceeds all previous records. But perhaps the most remarkable statement of all made by him in this connection is to the effect that for the 50 years, from 1831 to 1880, the world's consumption of gold " by the arts and manufactures exceeded its production $96,468,560."

During this period the world's output of gold was $4,245,579,000, and of silver $2,370,343,000, making a total of $6,615,922,000. If he will refer to Mulhall's " Dictionary of Statistics " under article " Plate," he will find that the amount of these metals consumed in the arts during this period, in Great Britain and France, which probably represented half of the world's consumption, did not amount to 10 per cent of the world's produce. (This, however, is probably too low. It is variously estimated at from 20 to 40 per cent, some even higher.) And again, if he will refer to the same work under the head of " Coin," he will find that this author states that the world's stock of coin in 1830 was £313,000,000, or say $1,565,000,000, while in 1880 it was £1,128,000,000, or $5,640,000,000, an increase of £815,000,000, or $4,075,000,000. If, then, the consumption in the arts during this period exceeded the entire production by $96,000,000, as Mr. Scott asserts, where did this enormous increase of " coin " come from ? It must be remembered, too, this is not only in excess of the consumption of the arts but of loss by abrasion, shipwreck and all other destructive causes.

Max O'Rell relates a story of an American visitor's description of things seen in Paris that he ought not to have seen, and the humorist, after intimating each questionable view, exclaims comically, "*Where did he go?*" After reading Mr. Scott's article I am constrained to ask, Where did he go in his little journey into the world of economics?

To go into the question of the world's precious-metal product, and of the influence it is supposed to exert over the products of labor and industry, I have not the time at present. But as the evident purpose of Mr. Scott's article is to show that existing economic maladies are attributable to "a scarcity of money largely due to the demonetization of silver," and "as the demonetization of silver depreciated its value, so remonetizing it will appreciate its value,"—if there is any principle of economic law governing such phenomena, Mr. Scott would undoubtedly confer a lasting obligation upon many earnest inquirers who, like myself, have been groping their way in search of truth through the bewildering maze of perplexing phenomena which surround this subject, if he will reconcile his theories of "Hard Times" as a result of the scarcity of money with the history of financial and industrial phenomena for the last forty odd years. And to assist him in such a task I will here furnish the necessary data so far as it relates to the "supply" of the precious metals to the Western world during this period, which approximately represents the "supply" of metallic money and its supposed effect upon "prices" and "general prosperity," only adding in advance that, so far as this country is concerned, the amount of money per capita at the important dates within this period was, in 1851, $13.76; 1873, $18.58; and in 1896, $31.20.

Period of High Prices, 1851 to 1865, 15 years.

World's produce of gold			$1,947,925,000
World's produce of silver	$601,122,000		
Less exports to Orient	752,948,675	loss	151,826,675
Gold and silver "stocked" by Western nations			$1,796,098,325
Average per annum			119,739,888

Period of Falling Prices, 1866 to 1894, 29 years.

World's produce of gold			$3,494,463,000
World's produce of silver	$3,419,450,000		
Less exports to the Orient	1,005,009,790		2,414,340,210
Gold and silver "stocked" by Western nations			$5,908,803,219
Average per annum			203,751,835
Average per annum 1851 to 1865, as above			119,739,888
Increase per annum (70 per cent)			84,011,947
Increase population per annum (1 per cent).			

When Mr. Scott shall have answered these and other queries already propounded in my article in your issue of February 29th, I shall be willing to offer more for his consideration. In the meantime I ask him to consider Lord Macaulay's observation on King James' luckless experiment in brass money for Ireland, as follows: "Public prosperity could be restored only by the restoration of private prosperity, and private prosperity could be restored only by years of peace and security," and, I will add, by honest, patient industry and frugality, and offer the suggestion that a Government cannot enrich its people by taxation, nor create values by legislative enactment.

[From News Letter, June 20, 1896.]

Editor News Letter :

SIR : As an American writer has recently said in a comparison of the past with the present, not only are we disposed always to look upon the past as a somewhat Arcadian period,—a period in which life and manners were better and more genuine than they now are, and as a sort of Golden Era when compared

with the present,—but there is usually a sense of
reverence, of filial piety, connected with it. Like
Shem and Japhet, approaching with averted eyes, we
are disposed to cover up with a garment the nakedness
of the progenitors; and the searcher after truth, who
wants to have things appear as they were, and does
not believe in the suppression of evidence, is apt to
be looked upon as a personage of no discretion and
doubtful utility.

A two and a half months' absence from the State
has prevented an earlier reference to Mr. Scott's
rejoinder, in the May *Overland*, to A Layman's comments on the statements, inferences and conclusions
in the "Hard Times" series of articles. The article
referred to abounds in errors, but the minor ones will
be passed over, because the more important are all
that A Layman has time to deal with.

In the number of the *Overland* mentioned, Mr. Scott
says :

"Charity suggests that Layman may be 'mad.' If
he be so, it would, in view of his utterances as to the
power of Government to create value by statutory
enactment, seem the acme of hyperbole to say, 'much
learning doth make thee mad!'"

And he otherwise disposes of A Layman's views with
a breezy assertion not unlike that displayed by Mark
Twain when he told an audience that he had selected
for discussion a subject with which he was not familiar
so that he might treat it unrestrainedly. As who
should say :

"I am Sir Oracle, supreme and infallible;
And the things I don't know, those things are not valable."

As to the power of Government to create value by legal enactment,—fiat,—A Layman's conception of which Mr. Scott thinks so feeble, amongst economists of distinction it is accepted as an axiom that law cannot create value, and no international bimetallists even, of repute, claim that power for Government ; they admit the contrary, but contend that Government can set in motion economic forces that will control value by controlling supply and demand,—thus in regard to silver upon the theory of general concurrence by the powers of the world. Archbishop Walsh, in his book on international bimetallism, says : " While legislation cannot directly give value to a thing, it can do so indirectly : it can set up a demand which is one of the factors of value ;" and Prof. Andrews, in his " Honest Dollar," says that " While law cannot control value independently of supply and demand, it can set free an economic force which will largely control supply and demand themselves." They distinctly declare that unlimited free coinage by any one Government would be disastrous. I have hitherto sufficiently shown that coinage does not operate as demand in its economic sense,—which implies a destruction of the material involved,—but is simply a hoarding of the metal. And it is certain that every attempt of Government to confer upon money a value at variance with the commercial value has proved futile through all time. If my conception of this fact indicates lack of learning, I am nevertheless in noble company,—Oresme, Copernicus, Gresham, Locke, Newton, Liverpool, Franklin, Morris, Hamilton, Jefferson, and other illustrious names.

I have no desire to commit Mr. Scott to something he does not believe in. If he is not in favor of the independent, unlimited free coinage of silver by the United States, I misconstrue his articles. If he is I do not, and am not alone. The construction placed upon them is shared by others familiar with the subject. If he is for free coinage and only objected to the ratio I named,—16 to 1,—what ratio does he favor? Within the century the commercial ratio has varied from about 15 to 1 to 34 to 1. Can a ratio be made which will measure all values and all debts and all credits on the basis of a fluctuating value like that?

As to the concurrent use of gold and silver in the United States from 1687 to 1873, which Mr. Scott alleges: If there was any appreciable current use in this country of either gold or silver in the seventeenth century, I have not found it recorded in history. Wampum, warehouse receipts, etc., were currency, beaver skins, corn, tobacco, rice, etc., were money of redemption, and pounds, shillings and pence the money of account, or book money, and so continued until well on into the eighteenth century. Mr. Jefferson, in 1805, discontinued the coinage of the silver dollar provided for by law in 1792, because depreciated foreign coins expelled the American coins, and for over thirty years not a dollar was issued. Our currency was either the paper of State banks, fractional coins, or depreciated foreign silver coins. The ratio of silver to gold, 1792–1805, drove gold out of circulation, and the depreciated foreign silver coins in turn drove the United States silver coins out. Here we have the

Gresham Law in duplex action. Hence Mr. Jefferson's order of 1805 to discontinue the coinage of silver dollars. For the baneful effects of depreciated money in the United States, see McMasters' History of the American people, wages, and prices of commodities, from 1770 to 1800. In Great Britain, by proclamation and mercantile concurrence, gold became the money of commerce in 1717, and has remained so for 180 years.

Mr. Scott reiterates his error regarding gold and silver,—that "A greater production of one or the other did not affect the parity established between them * * * and that from time immemorial gold and silver worked together harmoniously,"— and of A Layman's statement, that "Gold and silver never have circulated freely, concurrently and indiscriminately as coins at fixed ratios as legal tender under unrestricted coinage." He asserts that it "seems random and in conflict with the facts."

On page 526 Mr. Scott says:

"In 1834, on account of the greater cost attending the coinage of silver than gold of equivalent value, Congress made the ratio of silver to gold 16 to 1."

What is Mr. Scott's authority for that statement? It was the failure to circulate concurrently that caused the change to gold. The Congressional Committee appointed to investigate the subject reported as follows. The first report of 1831 says:

"That there are inherent and incurable defects in the system which regulates the standard of value of both gold and silver, its instability as a measure of contracts and mutability as the practical currency of a particular nation, are serious imperfections, while the impossibility of maintaining both metals in concurrent, simultaneous or promiscuous circulation appears to be as clearly ascertained.

" That the standard being fixed in one metal is the nearest approach to invariableness, and precludes the necessity of further legislative interference."

The second report of 1832 says:

" If both metals are preferred, the like relative proportion of the aggregate amount of metallic currency will be possessed, subject to frequent changes from gold to silver, and vice versa, according to the variations in the relative value of these metals. The Committee think that the desideratum in the monetary system is the standard of uniform value; they cannot ascertain that both metals have ever circulated simultaneously, concurrently and indiscriminately in any country where there are banks or money dealers, and they entertain the conviction that the nearest approach to an invariable standard is its establishment in one metal, which metal shall compose exclusively the currency for large payments."

That is to say, standard money, money of commerce. This conclusion is impregnable.

Congress, in the acts of 1834-37, designed to make the ratio such that gold would remain in this country, whether under it we could keep silver or not. This is familiar history. The object of this change was distinctly stated, especially by Mr. Benton, who said:

" To enable the friends of gold to go to work at the right place to effect the recovery of that precious metal which their fathers once possessed; which the citizens of European kings now possess; which the citizens of the young republics to the south all possess; which even the free negroes of San Domingo possess; but which the yeomanry of this America have been deprived for more than twenty years, and will be deprived forever unless they discover the cause of the evil, and apply the remedy to its root."

The official reports of French Government Committees subsequently investigating the subject for France were as follows. I extract from Professor Laughlin:

"An official document issued by the French Government in 1872 says that in 1808 the circulation in France was only about eight million francs of gold and two million of silver. In 1838 the whole of the French circulation did not include over five per cent of gold out of the total circulation of forty millions; that is, silver had driven out gold, because they were not at a parity.

"The same document says that, since the law of 1803, France has had no gold monetary circulation during the period before 1850. Up to that time silver was our sole monetary circulation, but, after the gold discoveries of California and Australia, gold took the place of silver in the general monetary circulation of the country.

"Again, in the report issued by the Minister of Finance in 1869, it is stated that in 1843, out of fifty-three million francs then possessed by the banks, only one million francs were gold. This metal had disappeared from 1803 to 1848, because it had enjoyed a premium which reached at that time 1½ per cent."

There are numerous references of the same kind to show that not in France was there a concurrent circulation of gold and silver, for the reason that the two were not kept at a parity. Every student of our own monetary system knows perfectly well that the same was true of the United States.

Says Prof. Francis A. Walker, the ablest international bimetallist in the United States:

" We flatly deny that bimetallism necessarily involves the concurrent circulation of the two metals. There is some reason to believe that the French statesmen of 1803 really expected that concurrent circulation would result; but no bimetallist nowadays makes the concurrent circulation of the two metals in the same country a necessity of that system."

Says ex-Secretary of the Treasury John Sherman:

" The two metals, as metals, never have been, are not now, and never can be, kept at par with each other for any considerable time at any fixed ratio."

As already stated, even the bimetallists do not claim that the two metals did or would circulate simultaneously, concurrently and indiscriminately. Mr. Scott's quotation of the law of 1792 fixing ratios only serves to make more manifest the weakness of his position. Gold was driven out from 1792 to 1834; standard silver was driven out in 1834, until Government coinage began in 1878. Not only was the law of 1792, as others of like character passed in the United States, futile, but those of Europe also; and in Europe they had been issuing similar kingly decrees for five hundred years, every one of which was as impotent as every other.

Alongside of Government or legal ratios there is always a commercial ratio that governs the purchasing power of money.

137

[*From News Letter, June 27, 1896.*]

Editor News Letter:

SIR : Recurring to the "Silver Question" and the "Hard Times" articles, which "A Layman" discusses from a purely historical and economical standpoint, Mr. Scott says : "From 1687 to 1873—one hundred and eighty-six years—our country employed both the silver and the gold dollar, equal one to the other as a standard of value *and redemption money.*" Where did the *gold dollars come from previous to 1785?* Pounds, shillings and pence were our money of account up to that date, two years after the independence of the United States was acknowledged. And it is estimated that at the time of the Revolutionary War there was not $1 per capita of gold and silver in the country. As to the circulation of gold and silver in Europe at a parity, if Mr. Scott were familiar with his subject he would know that in the larger commerce of Europe and the world the two metals passed by weight and not by tale. That is, they were subject to the mercantile value of money, as they are now in international commerce.

Mr. Scott, with all the naïvete of "Coin's Financial School," says : "During a period of 186 years the commercial ratio of silver to gold was never below 14.14, nor above 16.25." This is a variation of 14 per cent. Inconsiderable it was not. It was always easily sufficient to exclude from current circulation one or the other metal in the United States, as well as in France and elsewhere. But, no matter what the ratios were, the metals would not, never have, and never will, circulate freely, concurrently and indiscriminately as legal-tender coins under unrestricted coinage, except momentarily when crossing each other in their oscillations. Why? Because always and everywhere, since the dawn of civilization, commercial ratios have governed the coinage ratios in the purchasing power of coins, and the undervalued coin always goes to the melting pot, is hoarded or exported, while the overvalued is forced into circulation. Again, why? Because there is a margin of profit in such disposition,—brokerage. This is the Gresham Law. To quote the Duc de Noailles on the "Future of Bimetallism:"

"Who would not revolt at the idea of decreeing the obligatory equivalence of two constant quantities of wheat and oats, of cotton and wool, or iron and lead? Under such conditions no honest transaction would be possible, each of these several products being affected, respectively, by dissimilar and variable rises and falls. The force of solidarity of the products would cause inevitable injustice in exchanges. Why should an obligatory equivalence between two determinate weights of gold and silver be more practicable or more legitimate?"

"Value knows its own laws, and follows them despite kingly decrees or legal enactments." This was the reason why Great Britain followed the Petty theory in her legal action in 1815, subordinating silver, and why the United States, in 1853 and 1873, did the same. This reason for our legislation in 1853 was publicly stated in Congress by Dunham of Indiana,— because the only feasible bimetallism is gold as standard, silver as subsidiary or auxiliary. (*But the latter is justifiable and efficient only to such an extent as the people will actually use it ; beyond this it is a waste of capital.*) Alexander Hamilton said :

" There can hardly be a better rule in any country for the legal than the market proportion. The presumption in such case is that each metal finds its true level according to its intrinsic utility in the general system of money operation."

Hamilton also declared that, if the two metals at any time were separated, the more valuable one must be the standard, for the reason that the fluctuations would be more likely to attach to the inferior ; and he endeavored to adopt as the legal ratio the then commercial ratio between the two in the market of the world. To use his exact language :

" As long as gold, either from its intrinsic superiority as a metal, from its rarity, or from the prejudices of mankind, retains so considerable a pre-eminence in value over silver as it has hitherto had, a natural consequence of this seems to be that its condition will be more stationary. The revolutions, therefore, which may take place in the comparative value of gold and silver will be changes in the state of the latter rather than in that of the former."

In discussing monetary matters Thomas Jefferson said, as all the world's statesmen have said before and since, that the question of the difference between the value of gold and silver as money was purely a commercial question. It did not depend on legislation, or the fancy and taste of men, but on commerce, which regulates the price of commodities, and that "the whole art of Government consists in the art of being honest."

If silver as standard money is now going out of use in a natural way we cannot stop it, and the attempt to do so can only involve us in trouble. Moreover, the change is only a part and parcel of the vast—incalculable—economic change that modern invention and productivity have wrought within thirty years.

" The productive appliances of modern invention have put in operation forces, the magnitude of which we have not yet learned how to estimate, which we are not yet able to control, and the drift and final outcome of which we are unable to forecast. The expansion of productive force and mechanism has been so gigantic as to carry our capacity of output beyond our capacity of appropriation. The effects of these new conditions have been unforeseen; *and we have sought to protect ourselves against their consequences, when they have appeared, by extemporized expedients, regardless of fundamental economic principles and of the maxims which experience has shown to be wise and safe under any and all conditions.*"

Of this more anon.

" Layman " said in substance that the independent, unlimited free coinage of silver by the United States would be especially disastrous to wage-earners and depositors in savings banks. Mr. Scott remarks, " Layman seems to conjure up a fallacy, and then cries out against the creature of his own imagination," and Mr. Scott asserts that " the country demands the remonetization of silver." The State Conventions favoring silver—including the California Republicans and Democrats—have named the ratio of 16 to 1. At this ratio it would be silver monometallism, with a fifty-cent dollar; and, as to the status under such conditions, "Layman," being a gold-standard Democrat of the straightest sect of Jefferson, Jackson, Benton, Tilden and Cleveland, will offer Republican testimony: Said Senator Sherman of Ohio, in the United States Senate, February 27th:

" I believe in the use of both metals to as great an extent as is possible, at the same time maintaining their parity. In this country to-day the laboring man receives a dollar equal to gold worth 100 cents. But with free silver dollars the laboring man would be cheated of one-half of his dollar. The people are beginning to understand this. They are beginning to learn that free silver coinage means cheating the creditors out of one-half their dues. The maintaining of both metals as money should be such that each would be equal to the other. That would be true bimetallism. The adoption of free silver means silver monometallism, with half depreciated silver coin."

Andrew Carnegie of Pennsylvania is reported in the *Iron Age* for May as follows:

"Q. Do you attribute the great depression and panics that have occurred in the last few years to the agitation for a reduction in the standard of value?

" A. I do. All other causes combined have not affected the country to the extent that this has. It is fundamental; nothing is settled unless this is settled, and no genuine prosperity is possible. Capital at home, equally with capital abroad, has become alarmed. It has run into its hole, and will not come forth to embark in enterprises which create prosperity until it is settled that the American people borrowing $1 in gold will return $1, and not seek to defraud their creditors by returning a dollar worth only fifty cents."

Said ex-Senator Platt of New York, in the *Sun* of May 11th:

"The people of this country have had enough of the attempt to force fifty cents worth of silver into circulation as a dollar. They have suffered incalculable losses as the result of twenty years of that policy. Every business man knows that the line has got to be drawn sharply and distinctly against every public man whose words threaten the country and its business interests with any further debasement of the currency, or with any more of those losses and sacrifices which have followed every effort to force silver upon the country."

Marvin Hughitt of Illinois said at Chicago, May 30th:

"There can be no broad business development while the outlook of business men cannot go further than the gold reserve of the United States Treasury.

"Until we can look beyond that there is no need of expecting any widespread improvement in general business. The indications in some ways seem to be most encouraging to those who are looking for an early settlement of the currency question.

"When such States as North Dakota and South Dakota declare emphatically for a gold standard, there is reason to believe that we are getting through the process which a country with a government like ours must go through from time to time; that we are coming to our senses.

"On the other hand the Democratic party in this great State of Illinois appears to be dominated by men who want to pay their obligations with fifty-cent dollars."

In March the Secretary of the National Transportation Association of America spoke at Chicago as follows:

" Anything less than sound money, good everywhere on earth for its face, as the basis of our promise to pay, is either a fraud, a subterfuge, a financial cowardice, or a deliberate attempt to conceal the truth, or to stifle the financial conscience of the nation by shouts and appeals of demagogues, whose constituents pretend to fancy that fifty cents worth of something will buy a hundred cents worth of anything."

Says Murat Halstead:

" The silver controversy is unworthy the intelligence and the integrity of the American people. This free coinage of silver policy is a poor, shabby, half-way proposition. It is a fifty-cent repudiating dodge, or it is sheer craziness. If it does not mean to settle at fifty cents on the dollar, what is it fit for? Outside of this country, in the gold countries no one advocates what we call free coinage. Such madness of misinformation is not conceived of elsewhere."

In consonance with the foregoing views, the Republican party, in National Convention assembled at St. Louis, June 17th, declared as follows:

" We are unalterably opposed to every measure calculated to debase our currency or impair the credit of our country. We are, therefore, opposed to the free coinage of silver, except by international agreement with the leading commercial nations of the world, which we pledge ourselves to promote, and until such agreement can be obtained the existing gold standard must be preserved.

" All our silver and paper currency must be maintained at parity with gold, and we favor all measures designed to maintain inviolably the obligations of the United States, and all our money, either coin or paper, at the present standard, the standard of the most enlightened nations of the earth."

What is the present or existing gold standard? Although the Revised Statutes and Statutes at Large direct the issue and prescribe the uses, more or less limited, of several kinds of currency, to but one do they assign the office of a standard. To but one dollar do they assign the function of a unit of value. The function of a gold dollar as the unit of value is, therefore, unqualified and unquestionable. Its value is the unit of value. Its measure is made the only measure. To that measure every other dollar must conform, while other dollars exist, and this law of Congress stands.

[*From News Letter, July 4, 1896.*]

Editor News Letter:

SIR: I have said in these papers that the subject will be discussed by me from a purely historical and economical standpoint, and in doing so I shall frequently use the phraseology of standard authorities without in each and every case indicating the fact by quotation marks.

In the May *Overland* Mr. Scott says:

"The money lenders, money gamblers, etc., might perchance be adversely affected by the establishment of bimetallism."

(Meaning, I assume, the independent, unlimited free coinage of both gold and silver as legal tender at fixed ratios.) France holds as much silver as the United States, and the ratio there is 15½ to 1, but free coinage was long ago discontinued by France, and she declines to resume, maintaining, however, restricted silver circulation, practically on the Petty system or theory. If the United States accords independent, free, and un-limited coinage of silver, gold will be driven out of cur-rent circulation; and, with the parting of the two coins in circulation,—after the monetary panic is over, after the financial wreck,—comes the wreckage, comes the op-portunity of the money brokers, "money gamblers," etc., at the expense of the people. Vide greenbacks, gold and silver, 1862 to 1878.

Let it never be forgotten that a *coin is just as bad when debased by overvaluation, if not exchangeable for better, as when unduly alloyed, clipped or sweated.*

Adam Smith sets forth the condition of Hamburg, 1609, as follows:

" Before 1609 the great quantity of clipped and worn foreign coin, which the extensive trade of Amsterdam brought from all parts of Europe, reduced the value of its currency about nine per cent below that of good money fresh from the mint.

" Such money no sooner appeared than it was melted down or carried away, as it always is in such circum-stances. The merchants, with plenty of currency, could not always find a sufficient quantity of good money to pay their bills of exchange, and the value of those bills, in spite of several regulations which were made to prevent it, became in a great measure uncertain.

" In order to remedy these inconveniences, a bank was established in 1609 under the guarantee of the city. This bank received both foreign coin, and the light and worn coin of the country, at its real intrinsic value in the good standard money of the country, de-ducting only so much as was necessary for defraying the expense of coinage, and the other necessary ex-pense of management. For the value which remained after the small deduction was made, it gave a credit in its books. This credit was called bank money, which, as it represented money exactly according to the standard of the mint, was always of the same real value, and intrinsically worth more than current money. It was at the same time enacted that all bills drawn upon or negotiated at Amsterdam of the value of six hundred guilders and upward should be paid in bank money, which at once took away all uncertainty in the value of those bills. Every merchant, in consequence of this regulation, was obliged to keep an account with the bank in order to pay his foreign bills of exchange, which necessarily occasioned a certain demand for bank money."

The agio or discount on these moneys varied from 9 per cent to 14 per cent, and this, of course, had to be borne by the people who paid the coins to the merchants. There is an admirable exposition or treatise by Lord Liverpool, at the close of the last century, on a similar state of affairs in England. The circulating silver coins were at a discount, as against good money, of from 9 per cent to 38 per cent. This inequality is always the bane of the people.

Prof. W. A. Shaw, in his history of currency, speaking of the conditions prevailing in the sixteenth and seventeenth centuries, says :

" There was constant oscillation,—change of ratio; and the least alteration of the condition of one metal made it a lever for operations on the other. These operations were for brokerage commissions merely. They had no relation to the ebb and flow of commerce as modern arbitrage transactions have. It was a money dealer's opportunity of private gain, and for private gain the system was worked. The ebb and flow of European currencies, which the sixteenth and seventeenth centuries witnessed, were as unnecessary for the purposes of her commerce as they were disastrous."

A striking portrayal of the injury wrought by such causes is also to be found in the fourth volume of Macaulay's History of England, chapter twenty-one. He describes the baneful effect of the employment of clipped coins, which had become, in the year 1695, so universal that he says of it:

" It may well be doubted whether all the misery inflicted on the English nation in a quarter of a century by bad kings, bad ministers, bad parliaments and bad judges was equal to the misery caused by a single year of bad crowns and bad shillings."

It was found necessary to apply a remedy, and Somers, Montague, Locke and Newton were the men who devised measures for relief. The bad money was melted down and good substituted for it,—that which was worth as bullion what it purported to be as coin. Macaulay says that " in the midst of the public disasters one class prospered greatly,—the bankers." They were in a position to take advantage of the opportunities of profit which were presented to them. But, he remarks:

* * * " The laborer found that the bit of metal which, when he received it, was called a shilling, would hardly, when he wanted to purchase a loaf of bread, go as far as sixpence. The ignorant and helpless peasant was cruelly ground between *one class which would give money only by tale and another which would take it only by weight.*"

Let Mr. Scott note the remark, "*take it only by weight.*"

When Mr. Scott asserts that gold monometallism (meaning, I suppose, the gold standard of value, with silver auxiliary, as in the United States and France) renders money scarce, he makes a statement that is in defiance of all the facts of the case. There is more money, real and credit, per capita in France, Great Britain and the United States, and the world also, than ever before, and this, too, with a refinement, a facility of exchange, never before approximated. The scarcity or abundance of money is indicated by the rate of interest. Interest was never so low as at the present time. In California the savings bank rate of interest earnings has fallen six-tenths in twenty years, and throughout the United States 33 per cent in the same period.

As countries on a silver monometallic basis are cited by the advocates of free silver as more prosperous than the United States, the prosperity surely cannot arise from what Mr. Scott calls "plenteous money," the circulation per capita being, approximately, as follows:

United States..	Gold, silver and paper, *active*.	$23.60 per capita.
Mexico	Gold and silver............	4.95 " "
Japan........	Gold and silver............	4.00 " "
India........	Silver and paper............	3.33 " "
China	Silver....................	2.08 " "
Malayan Straits.	Silver....................	3.26 " "

The obligations of one country to another are not in the main paid in money but in the exchange of productions, and the final settlement of balances only is in gold or silver as commodities, at their commercial value per ounce. No money can enter this commercial realm as standard but true money, viz, that based on intrinsic equivalency. Only that which, after melting, is worth as bullion what its face previously purported, is true money,—not any other; and no legal enactment or kingly decree can alter this unwritten law.

"Commerce, from the dawn of 'civilization, has been the supreme arbiter of every system of monetary exchange. That system has either stood or fallen as it has conformed to or been in violation of the principles of justice and equity which commerce has declared. That declaration has been at all times, without a single exception, that in every metallic money there must reside such intrinsic and indisputable value as makes the stamped coin of the same value as a commodity of merchandise as the unstamped."

As to the proportion of obligations to gold, 49 to 1, alleged by Mr. Scott on page 564 of his May article, say for the United States, or for the State of California, or the world,—it matters not,—the conception of the functions of money therein indicated is worthy of "Coin's Financial School;" and, to illustrate the absurdity of it, I suggest to Mr. Scott that to gold he add silver; then the proportion of his despair to hope will be, not as 49 to 1, but as 49 to 2!

Herodotus gives an account of a Persian king who treasured up his revenue in this way: "He melts the gold and silver he receives, and pours it into earthen vessels. When the jar is full and the metal cooled, he breaks the jar. From these lumps, when he wants money, he cuts off what he needs." But modern finance is not like that. Davanzate thought the sum of all the gold, silver and copper in the world equaled in value all the other wealth of the world. But we know better than that. It is related of the father of Alexander Pope, the poet, that when he retired from business in London he carried to a retreat in the country a chest containing some 20,000 pounds sterling, and took out from time to time what was required for household expenses; and the historian records that it is highly probable that this was by no means a solitary case. But times and manners have changed since then.

The example of a " circus dollar " is a good illustration in point. The clowns and other employes arranged themselves in a circle, say twenty-five of them in all. No. 1 said to No. 2 : " I owe you $2.00 ; I'll pay you as soon as I can." No. 2 made this statement to No. 3, No. 3 to No. 4, and so on around the circle, No. 25 repeating it to No. 1. No. 1 shoved his hands into his pockets, and, with a look of pleased surprise, pulled out a dollar. Turning to No. 2 he said : " I didn't know that I had that dollar. Here's so much on account." No. 2 took the dollar, and, with a similar remark, passed it on to No. 3 ; and so it went around the ring, No. 25 passing it to No. 1, who received it with a smile and started to put it into his pocket; but, instead, he turned to No. 2 and said : " I didn't expect to be able to pay you the balance so soon, but here it is." And so the same dollar went around the ring a second time, finally coming back to No. 1, who, with a satisfied smile, put it into his pocket. If this be deemed an absurd exemplification of the rapid and efficient movement of money to cancel a disproportioned obligation, the caviler will find the same principle illustrated on page 63 of Professor Nicholson's "Money and Monetary Problems."

Mr. Scott seems to be unconscious of the great economic potentialities of the present century, particularly those of the present generation,—the transferability of capital, cash or credit, the so-called international loan fund, constituting a mechanism in obedience to which money moves freely wherever it is in best demand,—wherever it is supposed it will earn the most. As examples, Erlandger & Co., the European bankers of the Southern Confederacy, averred that, in response to their advertisement for bids on fifteen millions Confederate Government bonds, they received bids for over five hundred millions. When France needed money to pay the German indemnity, fifty-five banking houses of Continental Europe and Great Britian promptly responded with over one thousand millions of dollars. And on the sixty-two million bond loan of the United States for 1895 there were bids in London for over five hundred millions, and for the bond loan of 1896 there were bids in New York for over five hundred millions. Said Walter Bagehot, speaking of the French loan :

"The magnitude of it as a single transaction was indeed new, but it is only a magnificent instance of what incessantly happens; and the commonness of similar smaller transactions, and the amount of them when added together, are even more remarkable, and even more important than the size of this one ; and similar operations of the "loan fund" are going on constantly, though on a far less scale."

For the Russian loan of five hundred millions of dollars recently offered by the bankers of Paris, the press dispatches reported that the bids submitted aggregated five thousand millions of dollars.

If, for example, the United States—having prepared for other forms of circulating notes—were to retire greenbacks and Treasury demand notes, and thereby break the endless chain of Government redemption of greenbacks, and save all further need for bond issues, and were to ask bids for five hundred millions of gold on 3 per cent bonds, they would be immediately forthcoming. But if the independent, unlimited free coinage of silver be achieved in this country, the first effect of that will be widespread ruin, because it will occasion the exclusion from current use of the stock of gold coins of the country, and to replace these by silver coins would require thirteen years of the entire coinage capacity of the United States mints,—this, to say nothing of the results of instant contraction, consternation and disastrous panic from the sale of securities that would be occasioned by such a change. But suppose ultimate inflation through the medium of silver: Money, like property, is parted with for a consideration. No matter how many more coins there might be coming from the mints under free coinage, and going into the pockets of bullion owners, there would be no more coins in the pockets of the people at large, unless they had something to exchange for them. Secretary Gallatin once said :

" The want of money is the want of exchangeable or valuable property or commodities, and the want of credit. The man who says that he wants money could at all times obtain it if he had either credit or valuable commodities."

In 1785 Gouverneur Morris said: "The surest way to render money plenty is to bear the evils of scarcity. To make it plenty, according to the desire of some, would be, as in the continental time, to make it no money at all; for when it can be obtained without labor and found without search, it is of no use to the possessor. Those * * * therefore, who try to make money so plenty that the people may get it for nothing will find that their money is good for nothing."

When a question of equity is considered in connection with the stability of a standard, it is averred, by those who have examined the subject, that the average duration of ordinary debts is less than a year, and it has been shown by statistical investigation that the average life of land mortgages of whatsoever kind and character is less than four years. As gold resumption was legally declared twenty-three years ago, fixing the standard of our money, it is perfectly safe to say that the average life of all land mortgages has expired six times over within that period. Compare the value of Western wheat lands and Southern cotton lands per acre before the Civil War, and it will be found that, despite the depression of the immediate present, the lands are worth far more than they were then. Mulhall reports the value of farm lands of the United States as follows, pounds sterling figured at $5:

1860	$ 6,910 millions.
1870	8,430 "
1880	10,610 "
1890	12,790 " (estimated).

But to be as exact as possible I will take the United States Census returns as follows :

1850 . . $3,272,000,000, or . . . . $11 14 per acre.
1860 . . 6,645,000,000, or . . . . 16 27   "
1870 . . Omitted because of depreciated paper currency basis.
1880 . . 10,197,000,000, or . . . . $19 02 per acre.
1890 . . 13,279,000,000, or . . . . 21 31   "

As for corporations, railway mortgages for example, they are a part and parcel of the present civilization in every country on the face of the globe, and as they mature from time to time they are almost invariably renewed at a lower rate of interest; and so it goes on, and will go on forever, without an appreciable demand being made for cash payment or anything of the kind. The same principle applies to domestic enterprises and loans from savings or commercial banks. So long as the borrower has good assets he does not need to pay more than the interest maturing, because what the banks seek are responsible customers who are willing to use the funds which they manage, and by far the greater part of these funds belong to the working people.

As to banks and their obligations, even if any considerable proportion of the deposits were called for and obtained, the people in general would not know what to do with the money they had withdrawn. This is not assuming a lack of intelligence on the part of depositors, nor that they are exposed to no hazard, nor that bankers can provide against all contingencies. Ricardo remarks, what every thoughtful banker has observed, that:

" On extraordinary occasions a general panic may seize the country, when every one becomes desirous of possessing himself of the precious metals as the most convenient mode of realizing or concealing his property; *against such panic banks have no security on any system.*"

The very reason for the existence of deposit banking —essentially a development of the present century—is that the owners of money find it less risky, troublesome and expensive to place it in a bank than to keep it themselves. The safety of deposit banking is confidence, and this is partly the result of habit, and partly of the knowledge that anything like wholesale and simultaneous withdrawal is impossible, inconceivable; and thus confidence is maintained, although the fact is perfectly well understood that the amount of money in hand or within reach is as a rule small compared with the amount of deposits, while the aggregate of properly constituted banks is a prepared machine to carry capital in any direction.

[*From a Circular Issued by Secretary Carlisle.*]

Monetary Systems and Approximate Stocks of Money in the Aggregate and Per Capita in Ten of the Principal Countries of the World.

COUNTRIES.	Monetary system.	Ratio between gold and silver legal-tender silver.	Stock of gold.	Stock of silver.	Paper currency.	Per capita of circulation.	
						Gold.	Silv'r.
United States (a)...	Gold and silver.	1 to 15.98	$600,100,000	$625,600,000	$383,300,000	$ 8 41	$ 8 77
United Kingdom...	Gold............	....	b 580,000,000	115,000,000	c 113,400,000	14 91	2 96
France.............	Gold and silver.	1 to 15½	b 850,000,000	487,900,000	c 32,100,000	22 19	12 94
Germany	Gold............	....	b 625,000,000	215,000,000	c 60,400,000	12 21	4 20
Italy	Gold and silver.	1 to 15½	c 98,200,000	41,400,000	c 191,800,000	3 20	1 35
Austria-Hungary...	Gold............	....	b 140,000,000	120,000,000	c 204,300,000	3 22	2 76
Russia	Silver	1 to 15½	b 480,000,000	48,000,000	c 539,000,000	3 80	38
Australia	Gold............	....	b 115,000,000	7,000,000	....	24 47	1 49
Egypt	Gold............	....	b 120,000,000	15,000,000	....	17 65	2 20
Japan	Gold and silver.	1 to 16.18	c 80,000,000	84,300,000	....	1 95	2 05
Total	....	....	$3,688,300,000	$1,759,200,000	$1,324,300,000		

a July 1, 1896; all other countries, January 1, 1895.   b Estimate, Bureau of the Mint.
c Information furnished through United States representatives.

[*From News Letter, July 11, 1896.*]

Editor News Letter:

SIR: Recurring to Mr. Scott's articles on "Hard Times" in the February *Overland*, his astonishing error regarding the consumption of gold seemed difficult to equal, but it is a mild draft on human credulity in its misleading effect compared with the following in the *Overland* for May. In that issue he says:

"To pay in gold the interest for two years on the aggregate debt of this country would require not only the world's entire output of gold during the specified time ($400,000,000), but the world's present stock of $4,000,000,000 in addition."

Now $4,400,000,000 is the interest on $110,000,000,000 at 4 per cent. As Mr. Scott combines two years for his example, we must divide the amount, leaving a debt of $55,000,000,000, and an annual interest account of $2,200,000,000. If he can demonstrate that, for example, after a general clearance of counterbalancing obligations, this country owes $55,000,000,000, or anywhere near it, I will not wonder at his simile of wolves; assuredly the contemplation of such a state of things as he asserts must have put his mind into a condition similar to that of the skater pursued by wolves:

> "Over his shoulder, wild with fear,
> One hasty glance he steals,
> And all the wolves in Christendom
> Seem scampering at his heels."

Under like circumstances I should myself be disposed to say with the frontiersman, "The woods are full of 'em." But, before accepting as truth his construction, I must respectfully ask a definite bill of particulars. To whom and for what do we owe fifty-five thousand millions of dollars?

The November, 1895, bulletin of the Department of Labor estimates the total public and private debt of this country at $20,227,170,546. The principal items are as follows :

Railway companies	$5,669,431,114
Business and homes—lots	3,810,531,554
Farms, etc.—acres	2,209,148,431
Public debts of all kinds	2,027,170,546
National banks	1,904,167,351
Other banks	1,172,918,415
National, State and local taxes	1,040,473,013
Crop liens	650,000,000
Street railway companies	182,240,754
Canal, turnpike and bridge companies, etc.	114,208,078
Public water companies	89,127,489
Gas companies	75,000,000
Electric and telephone companies	49,992,565
Telegraph companies	20,000,000
Other debts—private	1,212,761,236
Total	$20,227,170,546

If the whole mass of business transactions, including the passing to and fro of debits (which are offset by credits), be Mr. Scott's estimate of the obligations of this country, I grant him a monopoly of that interpretation of the situation. Every debtor has a creditor, but the real debt of a country is the sum remaining after its credits are deducted,—the clearing-house balance, as it were, upon a general adjustment. For a given period the clearing-house balances in London showed, of coin used, only three-fourths of one per cent, and 99¼ per cent carried in bills, cheques and notes.

That England has loaned us money at lower rates than other countries would appear to be the head and front of her offending, illustrating the old adage : If you want to lose a friend, lend him money. If we are bankrupt and cannot pay, we ought to make an assignment for the benefit of all our creditors. That is the way an honest man does when he fails in business. He does not hide his property and offer fifty cents on the dollar. To use the language of a well-known French writer of to-day, M. Guibert of Paris:

"We will say nothing of the moral discredit which would be cast upon the United States by the adoption of a monetary system equivalent in respect of Europe to a declaration of legal bankruptcy. Let us look to the consequences which would infallibly be produced by the accession to power of the men who recommend this solution,—the independent, unlimited free coinage of silver. Financial disasters would follow close upon evil economic measures, and general poverty would appear, with the discontented, the intriguing and the ambitious in its train."

We now come to Queen Elizabeth's proclamation relative to base money, regarding which Mr. Scott remarks, "She evidently had no reference to silver, which was sound money," etc. As to legal tender in Queen Elizabeth's time, which, Mr. Scott infers, it was proba-. bly not known then in connection with gold and silver as we now understand it, Prof. W. A. Shaw remarks:

"From the thirteenth to the eighteenth century both gold and silver were actually employed in European commerce without any idea either of declaring or restricting the tender."

If Mr. Scott were familiar with his subject he would know that the money termed base *was* silver, but issued at coinage value or debased much beyond its commercial value, and, not being redeemable in good money, was therefore base, just as silver compared with gold would be to-day under unlimited free coinage at any ratio less than its market value. Mr. Scott doubtless knows that a Mexican dollar—unlimited coinage—contains six grains more silver than a United States standard silver dollar, but is worth only fifty odd cents in San Francisco, or any other commercial or financial center of a first-class power of the Western world. If he would like to know the monetary conditions under Henry VIII. and Edward VI. (a period of the most flagrant and notorious debasement of money by kingly fiat in English history), that caused Queen Elizabeth's proclamation, I can enlighten him. These potentates believed that kingly decree—law, fiat—could create values. What it did create was indescribable human misery. *I repeat, a coin is just as bad when debased by overvaluation, if not exchangeable for better, as when unduly alloyed, clipped or sweated.*

Probably the gain of the money metals by Spain from America in the sixteenth and seventeenth centuries was followed by a rise of prices in Spain, the modern exchange and credit system being then unknown; and what the other powers of Europe, including England, lacked in solid quantity they sought to make up for in fictitious multiplication, thus causing an extraordinary advance in prices by reason of the continual debasement and depreciation of the money.

From the time of Henry VIII., early in the sixteenth century, until in Elizabeth's reign, the debasement of

the coinage was peculiarly deplorable. Henry VIII.
reduced the amount of silver in a pound sterling from
2,663 grains: first, in 1527, to 2,368 grains; second,
1543, to 2,000 grains; third, 1545, to 1,200 grains;
fourth, 1546, to 800 grains; and in 1551, under Edward
VI., it was only 400 grains, or, at present mintage
value of silver, about $1.08. Under the depreciated
coinage, prices rose over 400 per cent, and business was
active with the tradesmen, brokers and "money gamblers," but not so with the working people. The historian Jacob says:

"It would naturally be imagined, at a time when
money was almost exclusively looked upon as wealth,
that an addition to it (supposed new metal from Spain's
stores) would have been hailed with joy;—that every
individual and each community would have been glad-
dened at the knowledge that they were becoming more
rich than they had before considered themselves.
The very reverse of this, however, appears to have
been the case, and complaints of distress were never so
frequent nor so loud as at the period we are now referring to. The rates of wages to day laborers do not
seem to have risen in the same proportion as the necessaries of life, and the laws passed under Elizabeth for
the relief of the poor are sufficient evidence of their
wretched condition."

Of which Queen Elizabeth later on took further
notice by reforming the coinage. In the midst of this
period Bishop Latimer inveighed bitterly against the
cruel injustice wrought upon the laboring classes, saying that:

"Poor men (which live of their labor) cannot, with
the sweat of their face, have a living, all kinds of

victuals is so deare,— pigges, geese, capons, chickens, egges, etc. These things with others are so unreasonably enhansed, and I thinke, verily, that if it thus continue we shall at length be constrained to pay for a pigge a pound."

And, as Latimer predicted, it came about that they did have to pay a pound for a pig; but as shown above the pound would be to-day only $1.08.

In Thorold Rogers' " Economic Interpretation of History " he says :

" The conclusion which I arrived at was that *payments were made by weight, and not, as now, by tale ;* that, whatever was the weight of pieces issued by the mint, a man who covenanted to pay or receive a pound of silver for goods, services or dues received 5,400 grains of silver up to 1527, and 5,760 grains afterward, and that this system lasted from the earliest records down to the reformation of the currency under Elizabeth."

Hence Macaulay's reference to the grinding of the peasant between the upper and the nether millstones, that is, the exacting by weight and paying by tale.

Mr. Scott says :

" That, on a gold basis, money in this country is scarce is evidenced by the fact that we by necessity issue bonds to the amount of hundreds of millions of dollars, obsequiously paying the bond-takers, mostly foreign, a large premium on the gold received from them."

Mr. Scott should know that the demand for gold of this country within the past four years, while in part caused by the need of it resulting from the general breaking down of speculative inflation in Argentina,

Australia and the United States, has been largely caused by the sale of various forms of American investment securities held by foreigners, because of the apprehension that we might try to pay a dollar of obligation in fifty cents worth of silver. As to the necessity for the sale of bonds by this Government recently to provide a supply of gold, that was owing to the vicious system of note issues by the Government. The law of 1878 compels the reissue of greenbacks, no matter how often redeemed, and under the workings of that law, and the incubus of silver certificates and Treasury demand notes,—an addition of 500 millions since the gold reserve was fixed at 100 millions,—our Government *must* be the purveyor of gold for all bond-brokers, " money gamblers," importing merchants, etc. The vice is in the laws of 1862 and 1878, compelling the issue, redemption and reissue, in endless iteration, of legal-tender paper money by the Government. In 1879, in the Congress of the United States, General Garfield said : " I fear there will never be any permanent safety to business so long as there is a greenback in circulation." I shall be glad to furnish Mr. Scott an exposition of this subject if he desires it. (For the exposition the reader will please see " *Currency*," page 90.)

[*From News Letter, July 18, 1896.*]

Editor News Letter :

SIR: Digressing for a moment from Mr. Scott's previous articles to refer to one in the July *Overland:* He sets afloat again a misquotation from Aristotle, which appeared in Henry Cernuschi's "Nomisma," published some sixteen or seventeen years ago, and which was exposed at the time, particularly so by Louis A. Garnett of this city in a "Monograph on Bimetallism," published in 1881. Mr. Scott, in his endeavors to maintain the fallacy that Government can create value, misquotes Aristotle as follows: "Money by itself has value only by law and not by nature." In support of this view he goes on to quote Professor Andrews of Brown University, but Professor Andrews has not yet attained to eminence as an economist, and his views cannot be accepted as authority.

Aristotle, in giving an account of barter and the origin of money as a medium of exchange, etc. (see an article on the "Natural Law of Money" in the July *Overland*), in speaking of the inconvenience of barter arising from the incommensurability of commodities, etc., said, substantially:

"For this reason men invented among themselves, by way of exchange, something which they should mutually give and take, and *which, being really valuable in itself*, might easily pass from hand to hand," etc.

Referring in his "Ethics" to this idea of the inherent value of money, he adds: "But with a view to further exchange, if we have no present need of it, money is, as it were, our security," etc., thus clearly recognizing the value-storing function of money when based upon inherent utility, from which exchangeable value arises. Elsewhere in his "Politics," in discussing *the various theories of money*, he says:

" Men sometimes suppose wealth to consist in the quantity of money which any one possesses, as this is the medium with which trading and trafficking are concerned. *Others, again, regard it* as a trifle, as having no value by nature, but merely by arbitrary compact," etc.

This is the passage which was misquoted by Mr. Cernuschi, and those who have followed him, including Mr. Scott, by omitting the very important words, "*Others, again, regard it,*" etc. By this omission it has been made to appear, latterly, as Aristotle's own theory of money, whereas he was merely stating the various theories of others that were current in his days.

Singularly enough—in view of the revival of this error—I have at hand a definition of good money by Mr. Cernuschi. He says :

" The coins which, being melted down, retain the entire value for which they were legal tender before being melted down, are good money; those which do not retain it are not good money."

Mr. Scott can try this test on Mexican silver dollars, and, according to the political lights of last week's National Convention at Chicago, we are to have the opportunity of testing upon a large scale the efficacy of Government fiat in creating values. Of this delusion and its causes, more in future papers.

Recurring to the " Hard Times " article of Mr. Scott in the May number of the *Overland Monthly*, on page 572 he says :

" The act of 1873, limiting the legal-tender function of silver to five dollars, tended to diminish prices still further, and has proven a canker, growing continuously more obstinate."

A Layman would be glad to hear further from Mr. Scott regarding such an act of 1873, of which he has not had prior knowledge. The act of 1853 limited the tender of subsidiary coin to $5, and the act of 1873 omitted the silver dollar from coinage. However, the United States have, since that date, acquired approximately 500 millions of legal-tender silver. And here I submit for Mr. Scott an unanswered conundrum by Professor Lexis:

" How has it been possible that the United States, which, from 1878 to 1893, issued more silver money or silver-covered notes than all the European States taken together had issued in a like period previous to 1893, and more than it would have been called upon to coin under a system of universal international bimetallism; how has it been possible that the United States, which produces annually $35,000,000 gold, and coins in correspondingly large sums, and which, moreover, has maintained in circulation 500 millions of paper currency,—and a superabundance of media of exchange,—has suffered from a perhaps still greater depression than that assumed to have been produced in Europe by gold monometallism, and that the prices of commodities of the United States, notwithstanding the Chinese-like isolation of its market by a protective tariff wall, have shown the same downward movement we find in Europe ? Is it not plain that the movement of prices which in two regions, with the conditions of the standard so entirely different, but which manifest the same effects and the same course of things, must have other causes than the demonetization of silver, which did not really begin in the United States until the repeal of the purchasing clause of the Sherman Act (November, 1893), but which has left 500 millions of credit money in circulation at its full nominal value ? "

Again, if circulating money quantities control the price of commodities, why have they fallen in Germany after that government received $1,000,000,000 of gold from France, the greatest sum ever possessed at any one period by all the German States combined, and probably a greater sum than ever was possessed by any one government at any one time ?

Again : after the year 1780 an enormous and long-continued rise of prices presents itself. And when they had reached their highest, about the years 1809–15, a still more surprising fall of prices commences, reaching its lowest point between 1845 and 1849. Between 1809 and 1849, prices fell in the ratio of 100 to 41. This was the period in which the alleged great international monetary regulator, the so-called French Bimetallic Act of 1803, was supposed to be at its highest state of efficiency.

The great tribulation is the fall of prices, and the contention a rise of prices. The rise of prices from 1780 to 1813 — thirty-three years — was undoubtedly caused by the withdrawal from quiet pursuits of life and the slaughter of millions of men through the destructive agencies of war. From 1813 to 1847 (a period of thirty-four years) peace, industry and invention held sway, and prices declined in the ratio of 41 to 100. In 1847–48 began the American-Mexican war, the revolutions of continental Europe, afterwards the imperial régime of Louis Napoleon in France, then

the British Indian mutiny, next the Crimean war of
the allied powers, England, France and Italy, against
Russia, then that of Italy and France against Austria,
and subsequently of Prussia against Austria; while for
the four years from 1861 to 1865 the American civil
war, unparalleled in magnitude, was waged, as was also
the struggle of the Mexican patriots against the French
and Austrian invaders. This remarkable period of
conflict was closed by the Franco-German war of 1870,
which had but a few months' duration. Here was a
period virtually of twenty-three years (1848 to 1870)
of constant war, and prices rose again. But in 1870
peace ensued throughout the wide world, and for a
quarter of a century an almost unbroken era of national calm and unprecedented industrial activity has
prevailed, supplemented by the invention and application of mechanical forces undreamed of in any period
in the march of the human race. Under these Titanic
influences the wage-earning capacities of mankind have
increased in gold-using countries, while prices of commodities have fallen; and why not? As illustrating
the effect of war on prices in the United States I quote
from Peletiah Webster. He says all authorities agree
that in 1784 the hire of workmen was twice as great as
in 1774. " On an average forty to fifty per cent more
can now (1784) be obtained for labor and country
produce than their current price was in 1774."

But is war, therefore, to be desired as an agency of
prosperous times ?

In the Chicago *Quarterly Journal of Political
Economy* for March, 1895, is to be found an article on

"Money and Prices" by a gifted California woman Miss Sara McLean Hardy, which would be a credit to any of the best economists of this country, and it is respectfully commended to Mr. Scott with the suggestion that he read, ponder and inwardly digest.

In this connection the following from Pierre des Essars, French economist, just published, is of present interest:

" The advocates of free coinage are wont to invoke the theory of prices, and to enlarge upon a supposed appreciation of gold resulting from a monetary contraction, which is not to be discovered by any examination of the matter made in good faith.

" Those who make the fall in prices the basis of their complaints, and attribute it to a monetary cause, must accept the burden of proving their case, for as yet no relation of cause and effect has been established between the alleged scarcity of gold and the decrease in prices of commodities. What is incontestible is that industrial nations have been, and are, employing all the resources of modern science to reduce to the minimum the cost of production, and, as fast as an oversupply has closed the outlet for a constantly increasing capital, the money thus released has sought employment in new countries, which, in their turn, have become competitors of the old.

" *The attempt to use depreciated currency as a weapon with which to oppose a fall in prices, acting like one of the forces of nature everywhere and upon all substances, is simply an attempt to impede the evolution of humanity, and to place in jeopardy the future of civilization.*"

As a rise in prices is one of the things that the free silver advocates are clamoring for, let us inquire into that. As far as business activity—so-called prosperity

—is based on a greater quantity of production, *and that of the right article*, as far as it is based on the increased rapidity with which commodities of every kind reach those who want them, its basis is good. But in so far as that activity, or so-called prosperity, is based on a general rise of prices, it is imaginary, it is bad. A general rise of prices is a rise only in name. As a rule, with exceptions, whatever any one gains on the article which he has to sell, he loses on what he has to buy, and so he is just where he was. To the country, as a whole, a general rise of prices in domestic commerce is no benefit at all; it is simply a change of nomenclature for an identical relative value in the same commodities.

The status of recent land values in California and present depression offers a striking example of this:

Year.	Total number of farms.	Total acreage.	Improved.	Unimproved.	Total valuation of land, fences and buildings.
1850	872	3,893,985	32,454	3,861,531	3,874,041
1860	18,716	8,730,034	2,468,034	6,262,000	48,726,804
1870	23,724	11,427,105	6,218,133	5,208,972	141,240,028
1880	36,934	16,593,742	10,669,698	5,924,044	262,051,282
1890	52,894	21,427,293	12,222,839	9,204,454	697,116,630

The rate per acre is as follows : 1850, $.99 per acre ; 1860, $5.58 per acre ; 1870, $12.36 per acre ; 1880, $15.79 per acre ; 1890, $32.62 per acre, or an increase of 106 per cent per acre between 1880 and 1890 ; a total increase in values of $435,000,000, or 160 per cent, an inflation wholly out of proportion to any normal conditions or progress. Does Mr. Scott wonder that there should have been a collapse in values within the past six years ?

The above data was received from Edwin F. Smith, Secretary of the State Board of Agriculture at Sacramento, and Mr. Smith remarks:

"The value of farming lands in California at the present day has shrunk at least 25 per cent from the value of 1890 for many reasons. The first and most prominent one is that in 1890 the lands of California assumed a fictitious value by reason of the extension of fruit-growing. For a few years prior to 1890, the prices received for fruit warranted an increased acreage, and, to that end, the most valuable lands, namely, those bordering upon or near our large watercourses, or susceptible to irrigation, were in demand, and values increased. This fact enhanced, to a considerable extent, lands not susceptible to fruit culture, but that were situated adjacent to first-class fruit-growing land, and upon which cereals were cultivated. Under this influence these lands that were quoted at from $25 to $40 per acre increased to $50 and $75, not from any cause other than above quoted. It was about at this time that farmers began to feel wealthy, and invested in outside ventures, borrowing money upon these inflated values, and did not feel their condition until the present times of depression, and, when called upon to pay mortgages, found that transfer of loan was impossible by reason of shrinkage in values, and were, consequently, left in a deplorable condition."

The facts and opinions furnished by Mr. Smith are commended to Mr. Scott's careful consideration, for they will explain one of the chief causes of financial embarrassment among the California farmers.

Since the so-called demonetization of silver the gain of capital in the hands of the people, as shown by

deposits in savings banks in this State, has been
approximately as follows:

```
1870 about ...........................$  36,000,000
1880..................................    52,000,000
1890..................................    94,000,000
1895..................................   125,000,000
1896..................................   132,000,000
```

Any fair consideration of the land values and money
savings of this State will show how unfounded is the
cry of exceptional depreciation. There has been depreciation, but there was first inflation. We are to-day the
richest community per capita of any State in the world
—about $2,100 per head.

Mr. Scott says that at the close of the Civil War in
1865:

" Labor pressed upon the industries far in excess of
their ability to meet immediately its requirements. The
price of labor largely governing the price of various
commodities necessarily fell."

Now Mr. Scott's general contention is a fall of prices
because of a lack of money and lack of high protection.

Within a period, say from 1866 to 1877 inclusive, the
value of the average product of the precious metals in
this country was unprecedented, an average of over
$68,000,000 per annum, and yet during that period we
experienced the most extraordinary commercial activity,
and suffered, 1873-77, first, a financial panic, and second, an industrial stagnation, and third, a general
depression of business that has not been exceeded in
the history of the country, not even by the present,—

this during General Grant's two terms in office. Were these phenomena due to lack of ample protection and lack of money? Moreover, the period of falling prices has been the period of increasing wages up to 1893.

As to low prices, the history of our trunk-line railroad rates furnishes an interesting study. I quote from the Hon. John Dalzell, M. C., of Pennsylvania:

"In 1865 the Pennsylvania R. R. Co. and its lines west of Pittsburg; the New York Central & Hudson River R. R.; the Lake Shore & Michigan Southern; the Michigan Central; Boston & Albany; the New York, Lake Erie & Western, carried 11,151,701 tons of freight, or, to express it in another way, moved of tons, one mile, 1,654,324,000. And how much did each ton cost for carriage? It cost twenty-nine mills per mile. In 1885, twenty years afterward, the same system of railroads moved of tons, at the rate of one mile, 11,331,306,-000, at a cost of six mills a mile."

And reductions have continued since that time to the present.

A statement in the *Financial Chronicle* of June 6, 1896, of the business of the Southern Pacific Company, 1872 to 1895 inclusive, shows that, while the carriage of all business per ton per mile increased 80 per cent, the reduction in the receipts per ton per mile, from 1872 to 1895 inclusive, was 66 per cent, and this is not far from the rate of reduction general throughout the country during the same period. It seems pertinent here to add that the reports of our Interstate Commerce Commissioners show that railroad service in the United States costs the public on an average less than one-half what it does in Europe. Does Mr. Scott consider these reductions, which are universal, a hurt to the people? I believe that they are blessings, however much temporary disturbance or discomfort such vast changes impose.

Mr. Scott says:

" Congress, in 1873, largely deprived silver of its monetary use, and in consequence its value greatly depreciated. Should Congress confer upon silver a monetary use, the logical conclusion is that *its value would be augmented commensurate with such additional use.*"

I will again remind Mr. Scott that coinage is not demand in the economic sense of consumption, but is in fact storage,—stocking of supply; that the money metals only go to the mints when not wanted elsewhere. And this fact has two striking examples in this generation: First, the extraordinary gold coinage by the French Government in the fifties, which in one year coined more than the whole world's production for that year. Yet gold declined in value. Second, the Bland-Allison Act, in force from 1878 to 1890, authorized the purchase of from twenty-four to forty-eight million dollars of silver. July 14, 1890, the so-called Sherman Act, authorizing the purchase of fifty-four million ounces of silver per annum, was passed, very greatly augmenting the acquisition of silver. Yet from the time the law went into effect until it was repealed—three years and four months—the fall in the average price of silver was over 40 per cent. Says Senator Sherman, the author of the proviso:

" The act of 1890 demonstrated the inevitable result of free coinage in our country. If the purchase of 54

million ounces of silver a year did not prevent the
further decline of that metal, what would have been
the result if we received and coined all the silver that
would be brought into the United States from any
region of the world at the fixed rate of $1.29 per ounce,
worth in the market 73 cents an ounce? This is a
proposition the logic of which it is impossible to avoid."

There has been an extraordinary increase of the
British gold product within the past five years, including 1896, and it is more plentiful than ever in the
English and continental banks; and yet, as a matter
of fact, the coinage, which is free, has fallen off. Thus
the theory of the bimetallist is again put to the test,
and shows that it is unfounded. In fact, as stated
hitherto, coinage is not demand in the economic sense.
Moreover, it is the range of prices and the activity of
trade which determine the quantity of money in circulation, and not the quantity of money in circulation
that determines prices.

As to any possible benefit from the independent, unlimited free coinage of silver by the United States, Dr.
Otto Ahrendt, the eminent German bimetallist, says,
in the *North American Review* for June :

" The United States alone cannot establish the
double standard by adopting free coinage; they would
shift over to the silver standard, and we should vainly
wait for a stable ratio of values."

This is concurred in by every international bimetallist
of any repute whatsoever; and, I repeat, *a coin is just
as bad when debased by overvaluation, if not exchangeable for better, as when unduly alloyed, clipped or sweated.*

Political hysteria and popular frenzy may overthrow
established institutions, but they cannot overcome natural law.

[*From News Letter, July 25, 1896.*]

Editor News Letter :

SIR: Recurring to Mr. Scott's article in the February number of the *Overland*, referring presumably
to the indebtedness of our people, Mr. Scott likened
the condition of the country to a household at the
doors of which there were countless packs of ravenous
wolves, yet at the conclusion of his May article he
quotes Edward Atkinson to show that, since 1860 say
to 1894 (chiefly from '78 to '94, under the gold standard), the condition of the mechanics of this country
has been so improved that there is a net average gain
in the lower cost of necessaries and the higher price of
wages of $372 per year, or 54 per cent. This has
mainly resulted since 1878, under resumption and gold
standard; and similar improvement is just as marked
in Europe, notably France, but particularly in Great
Britain, a gold-standard, free-trade country. How does
Mr. Scott reconcile these increased wage-earnings with
that presumably famishing condition which, according
to his rhetoric, has filled the country with ravenous
wolves? Mr. Scott says further:

" *The workman's standard of measurement is his
labor.* To him the instrument of exchange—silver or
gold—between his labor and requirements is insignificant. Probably in most cases his convenience would
prefer payment part in silver and part in gold."

This latter is doubtless correct under the present status, but surely Mr. Scott knows that under the independent, unlimited free coinage of silver the workman would get no gold,—silver only, and that would be worth no more in its purchasing power than its silver bullion value; then it would by no means be an insignificant question, but, on the contrary, one of vital importance to every wage-earner and savings bank depositor, and under such a state of affairs a simile of wolves might become peculiarly pertinent. I repeat, *a coin is just as bad when debased by overvaluation, if not exchangeable for better, as when unduly alloyed, clipped or sweated.* Prof. Arthur T. Hadley of Yale College, in his " Economics," points out the evil effects of such a coinage, and calls attention to the fact that so ancient an observer as Aristophanes commented upon the tendency of depreciated money to drive out good, full-value money. I have already called attention to the conclusions of Oresme, Copernicus and Gresham in the fourteenth, fifteenth and sixteenth centuries, now known as the Gresham Law; and Professor Hadley, in commenting upon the Gresham Law, says, amongst other pertinent observations :

" As the amount of debased money grows larger, its sphere of usefulness grows smaller. Importers and others engaged in foreign trade have to provide themselves with a certain amount of cash reserve which derives its value from something more wide-reaching in its effects than a legal-tender act. Far-sighted capitalists, who fear the future fiscal policy of the Government, insert stipulations in their loans or in their leases requiring payment of dues in some specific

commodity rather than in the general currency of the
country. Even as a medium of exchange in domestic
transactions, the debased money may be discredited by
the action of the people. D'Avenal has collected some
curious facts which show that the arbitrary changes in
coinage made by the French crown were to a large
extent rendered inoperative in this way."

As Mr. Scott quoted Edward Atkinson I will also
put Mr. A. in evidence, as follows :

" The mass of gold in existence has been sufficient
to enable Germany to adopt the gold standard of legal
tender, the United States and Italy to resume specie
payment substantially on a gold standard, the Latin
Union to cease silver coinage and to maintain their
existing stock of legal-tender silver at par in gold,
without creating any apparent scarcity of gold and
without any special influence in depressing the prices
of commodities or services.

" The reduction in the price of commodities has
been no greater than would be warranted by and might
have been expected from the improvements in the pro-
cesses of production and distribution. This reduction,
having been accompanied by a general maintenance or
rise in the price or rate of wages, has been almost
wholly beneficial,—temporary hardship to special
classes being admitted.

" The advocates of silver monometallism disregard
the fact that, from the date of the resumption of specie
payment on a gold basis, January 1, 1879, to the date
of the silver panic in 1893, the fall in prices had been
accompanied by a constant rise in wages.

" The demand for more money in legal-tender notes
or silver dollars is made by persons who have no conception of the true conditions of trade. In their mis-
directed efforts to provide by legislation for the issue of

fiat money, or by free coinage of silver, they have created distrust, and have thereby brought on a panic accompanied by a partial paralysis of trade, thus reducing prices by their effort to increase them.

"The effort of the advocates of the free coinage of silver, or of the issue of Government legal-tender paper and other devices for supplying money, may be attributed to their ignorance of the function of credit and of the necessity for an established unit of value. Their efforts are usually accompanied by bitter prejudices against banks and bankers. The invariable result of any success on their part is a paralysis of industry by which prices are forced below cost, and the compulsory idleness of large numbers of workmen ensues. These results, long before predicted, were fully realized in the purely financial panic of 1893, and will be brought about again sooner or later unless the delusion of ' cheap money ' is crushed out."

Referring to Mr. Scott's apprehension that the perpetuity of the institutions of this country is threatened by the concentration of wealth : I would be glad to have him explain how the unlimited free coinage of silver—the foisting of a depreciated money on the people—would change a tendency to concentration. If he can do so he may thereby become a public benefactor. A depreciated currency invariably robs wage-earners. As pertinent to this I quote extracts from the State platform of the Socialistic party of Illinois, May 30th :

" The economic evils from which the people suffer are not caused by the gold standard. The free coinage of silver at 16 to 1, or at any other ratio, can in no way better their condition."

And the Socialist Labor party of California has declared, and declared wisely, as follows:

" *Resolved,* that we disapprove of the free coinage of silver at a ratio of 16 to 1, by the United States, as being class legislation for the debtor class, detrimental to the interests of the wage-earners, tending to further despoil the producers by cheapening their labor and reducing their purchasing power."

In the July *Overland* Mr. Scott says:

" No inconsiderable portion of our foreign commerce, amounting in 1890 to $1,600,000,000, is with silver-standard countries, the Orient and Spanish America. This will evidently from now on vastly increase. The prospects of rapid development of the immeasurable resources of those countries are bright with promise. In effecting those developments, their demands upon our markets for ships, railroad material, machinery and other products will be immense. Our commerce with Europe, so far as imports are concerned, will necessarily greatly diminish as we enlarge and perfect our manufactures. Wisdom, therefore, dictates that we cultivate commercial relations more assiduously with the silver-money countries than with the gold. Their markets are ours by nature, and will be so in practice if we are discreet and energetic. They are at our doors, while wide oceans intervene between them and our competitors. Our geographical position defies competition. Our monetary policy, so far as our foreign commerce is concerned, should be shaped in accord with these advantages. From a foreign commercial standpoint it would be better for us to adopt the silver-money standard rather than the gold, but better still for us to adopt the bimetallic standard."

What does Mr. Scott deem a bimetallic standard, and how would he carry it into effective operation ?

In the July *Engineering Journal* Edward Atkinson says :

" We have sold to the machine-using, gold-standard nations—Great Britain and her colonies, France, Germany, Holland and Belgium—our excess of food, fibres and fabrics to the extent of 83 per cent of all our exports. The gold value of our exports (mainly consisting of the products of agriculture) in the last decade, in excess of our imports from these specific countries, has been, in round figures, $2,500,000,000. The advocates of the free coinage of silver dollars of full legal tender propose to enable the bankers of Europe to gather in the silver bullion of the world, of which the market value is now 68 cents per ounce, to send it to our mints to be coined without charge, and then to force it upon our farmers, wage-earners and other persons at $1.29 per ounce, thus cheating them out of about half their dues for the benefit of two privileged classes,— the silver miners of the West and the foreign bankers and their agents of the East."

Will Mr. Scott please tell us what will become of our farmers if they lose their customers in Great Britain and Continental Europe ?

On page 366 of the February *Overland* Mr. Scott says of A Layman's criticisms :

" As to force in disproof of the accuracy of any statement of mine, he might as well have offered a handful of any other figures indiscriminately gathered; and perchance they would have been as creditable to him, as appears by the following: Thus he sets forth as a fact that the commodity value of the silver yield of the

United States in 1895 was approximately $36,000,000, as measured in gold; further, with respect to the world's output, he says: ' We find reference to authorities that the production of gold in 1895 was $200,000,-000, and of silver $120,000,000.' And so on he regales us with his statistics, as if really authentic. On application to the mint of the United States at San Francisco for the Mint Director's Report of the production of gold and silver in the United States in 1895, the statistician replied by letter: ' The Report is not yet printed,—is not yet prepared. When the Report is at hand for 1895 will send it to you.' So it would seem that Layman must have a statistics manufactory whose products are prophetic and not historic, as he would have us believe."

I beg most respectfully to suggest to Mr. Scott that the Mint Bureau of the United States is not the only repository of information, but that, if he will take the Bureau's figures for 1895 when they do appear, he will find A Layman did not exaggerate.

However, I further submit to Mr. Scott that my information for the United States of America, the Republic of Mexico, and for South Africa, was authentic; that for Russia and some minor producing points was estimated upon the basis of previous production. If Mr. Scott is still skeptical upon the subject, he will find, by referring to the press dispatches of December 20, 1895, a forecast with estimates from Director Preston, Washington, of the probable production; and A Layman takes the liberty of saying that his own estimates were lower in every case than those of the Government officials; and he repeats that if Mr. Scott will examine the 1895 Mint Report, when it is published complete, he will find A Layman's statements amply verified. The French economist, Paul Leroy Beaulieu, has stated the world's product of gold for 1895 at $200,000,000; the New York *Evening Post* gave it as $199,500,000; while the Mint Report now ready for publication states it at $203,000,000; and for 1896 the New York *Journal of Commerce* stated, July 9th, upon reports from the Mint Bureau, that the probable product of the present year will be $220,000,000.

Again, on page 565 of the *Overland*, Mr. Scott quotes the silver product of 1889 from Wells, Fargo & Company's statement on page 289 of Mint Report for calendar year 1894, and remarks:

" Nothing on the page indicates that these amounts were obtained for equal weights of the metal. No other inference can be drawn from the data than that the mint rate, $1.2929 per ounce, obtains in both cases. It cannot be inferred from the data given that the statistician meant otherwise."

Had Mr. Scott read the preceding—opposite—page (288) of the same report he would have seen it distinctly stated that the output of silver for 1894 had been estimated at the average commercial ratio for that year, or 63 cents per ounce. And I will add, further, that, had Mr. Scott desired official information on this point, the same Mint Report would elsewhere have enlightened him. On page 17 a table is given of the " Product of Gold and Silver, from Mines in the United States, 1873–94," compiled by the Mint Bureau of the Government. Moreover, the amount reported by Wells, Fargo & Co. in round figures, say $29,000,000 commercial

value, is less than that reported on page 17 of the Mint
Report. Of Mr. Scott's errors, which are the rule and
not the exception, more anon.

> "If a man could but sharpen his wits
> With the ease that he sharpens his knife,
> He would make some remarkable hits,
> Now and then, in the course of his life."

[*From News Letter, August 1, 1896.*]

Editor News Letter:

SIR: Recurring to the "Silver Question" and the
"Hard Times" articles by Mr. Scott, we note, in pass-
ing, his tribute to protection, on page 568 of the May
Overland, and his assertion that

"The record of facts shows that in this country, from
1620 to the present time, each and every period of nonprotection of home industries has been fraught with
adversity, and that each and every period of protection
of home industries has been fraught with prosperity."

I frankly confess that I do not understand what relation the status of the American colonies from 1620 to
1776 (over a century and a half) bears to the Republican policy of high protection; and it is certain there
has been no period of nonprotection in the last half
century. Moreover, the workings of the Walker tariff,
from 1846 onward, were so satisfactory than ten years
later, in the National contest of 1856, there was no
agitation of the subject, and practically there was no
interruption of the status from 1846 to 1862, after
which the Morrill tariff, confessedly a war measure,
went into effect. Moreover, the financial crash of 1873
and the subsequent industrial stagnation and business
depression of five years was in the period of an

extremely high tariff. The same applies to the break-down in 1882–85.

Of all the schemes for exaction from the people since the Civil War closed, that of extreme protection has been the most effectively "worked" up to the present time, and, combined with the issue of legal-tender paper money by the Government, is the legitimate progenitor of the silver craze, which, if carried to unlimited free coinage, will prove to be the greatest calamity that has ever befallen this country. That form of State socialism called protection has done more to foster class legislation and produce inequality of fortune, to create false standards in the popular mind and familiarize it with State aid and guardianship in private affairs, than any other single cause. And the evil effects are to be seen in the socialistic, not to say communistic, tendencies now shown by political parties, — not merely the Socialist and Populist parties, etc., but the Republican and Democratic parties. In the press dispatches of July 4th, amongst others of like tenor concerning the political situation and convention at Chicago, appeared from the Governor of a State what reads in part as follows :

"The East has, by legislation that makes us pay tribute to it, acquired what money there is in the country. We ask that the tariff shall be framed with reference to revenue for the Government and not for the purpose of making us pay tribute to the East."

Says Henry George in the dispatches of the 8th, commenting on Governor Altgeld's speech before the Democratic National Convention at Chicago :

" He spoke without evasion or equivocation of what is the real root of the silver movement in the agricultural West,—the desire to scale down debts,—raising, more clearly than any one I have hitherto heard, the banner of the ' House of Want ' against that of the ' House of Have.' "

Said Amos Cummings of Altgeld :

" He commanded the closest attention and made the most logical and attractive speech yet heard in the Convention."

The protection policy has been to not make the receipt of revenue the main consideration, but allow that primary object of fiscal regulations to be thwarted by the attempt not only to protect but to specially " promote " a great variety of particular interests at the expense of revenue, and of commercial intercourse with other countries. Adam Smith contended that labor was the one source of wealth, and it was by freedom of labor, by permitting the worker to pursue his own interest in his own way, that the public wealth would best be promoted; that any attempt to force labor into artificial channels, to shape by laws the course of commerce, to promote special branches of industry in particular countries, or to fix the character of the intercourse between one country and another, is not only wrong to the worker or the merchant, but actually hurtful to the wealth of a State. He also said: " There is no art which one government sooner learns of another than that of draining money from the pockets of the people." Or, as Walter Bagehot said: "All governments like to interfere; it magnifies their importance to make out that they can cure the evils of mankind."

Of the excessive and indefensible purchases by Government of silver as a sop to the Populists, I will again call in Republican testimony, lest Mr. Scott deem my view "a railing accusation void of truth." The Chicago *Tribune*, the leading Republican paper of Illinois, said, editorially, May 29th:

"The Sherman proviso was a cowardly makeshift. It was worse than that: it was a shameful trade. It was the costly price paid Teller and his fellow free silverites to secure the passage of the costly tariff bill of 1890. The Teller and Jones stripe of Senators refused to let the McKinley bill pass the Senate unless the other Republican Senators would pass the Sherman amendment, which was almost as bad as free coinage. And it brought on the country the disastrous panic of 1893."

This is one example of the workings of what Layman characterized as the legitimate result of pernicious economic methods in commerce and finance, namely, of the delusion that the Government can create value by statutory enactment and make the people rich by taxation. I repeat, the trouble in this country is not a lack of money, but, in part at least, of a sound economic and financial policy, which has, since the Civil War, been an almost unbroken record of empiricism, carried on in wanton disregard of the best established inductions of science.

As Mr. Scott quotes Daniel Webster in regard to labor, I will also put Mr. Webster in evidence. Said he in Congress:

"How, sir, do shipowners and navigators manage? How is it they are able to meet and in some measure to

overcome universal competition? Not, sir, by protection and bounties, but by unwearied exertion, by
extreme economy, by unshaken perseverance, by that
manly and resolute spirit which relies on itself to protect
itself."

It is an axiom in trade that the prices of exportable
products are fixed in the foreign market where the surplus is sold, and in the currency of that country according to its nominal value there. The California farmer
(whose obligations, mortgages *if there be*, are in terms
of gold) clamoring for free silver and what politicians
call the " Protection of American Industry," is a political spectacle for gods and men. Free to vote as they
like, yet voting to tax themselves for the benefit of a
protective tariff, while they sell their grosser products,
as to the excess left after home needs have been satisfied, on the basis of the price in Liverpool,—in competition with the world. Mr. Blaine asserted that the
McKinley bill did not provide a market for a bushel of
wheat or a barrel of pork!

It is customary for silver advocates to dwell, as a
writer in the *Overland* for July has done, upon Ernest
Seyd's prediction of impending hard times. Every period
of advance in the present century—the most remarkable
in its world-wide achievements in the history of the
human race—has been followed by a period of depression and temporary stagnation. For example, the
activity from 1819 to 1825—namely, that which resulted
from the resumption of specie payments by Great
Britain and the United States—was succeeded by the
breakdown of 1826, in which France also was involved.
Recovering from this, another onward movement was

made which culminated in the crash of 1837 to 1842; then came six years of great prosperity, followed in turn by a break in 1847–48, from which, however, all quickly recovered; and another period of marked prosperity ensued which lasted until 1857, when again a crash took place, the recoil of which was lost in the convulsions of the Civil War. Another break occurred in 1864–66; then, after a period of phenomenal activity from 1868 to 1873, we suffered a collapse and extreme depression from 1873 to 1877. The renewed activity, 1878 to 1882, met with a reverse upon the death of President Garfield, which continued some four years, and, after an extraordinary revival of prosperity during the eight years from 1885 to 1893, came the crash from which the country is still suffering.

As a matter of fact there is no logical connection whatever between these periods of feverish activity and subsequent collapse and depression, and silver or the policy of protection, beyond the pernicious, the noxious, effect of artificial stimulus to prices,—speculation and industrial exploitation,—because such periods of activity and depression have manifested themselves in Great Britain as well as France, and Great Britain and her colonies have progressed as we have. Nor have circulating money quantities had any appreciable effect, except as they departed from the true standard of value, —intrinsic equivalency,—thereby making commodities high in the ratio of money depreciated below the true standard of value, as witness France during the Revolution, etc., England during the continental wars, and the United States during the Revolution and our Civil War.

Mr. Gladstone has stated that the amount of transmittible wealth,—that which could be handed down to posterity,—produced during the first eighteen hundred years of the Christian era, was equaled by the production of the first fifty years of this century, and that an equal amount was produced in the twenty years from 1850 to 1870. What of the period from 1870 to 1896? If we take railroads, iron steamships, electric power, and improved manufacturing plants, these last twenty-five years have exceeded all the rest. Of the railroads and iron steamships at present in existence, 70 per cent have been constructed since 1870. It is alleged that twenty years ago the power of machinery in the mills of Great Britain was computed to be equal to 600,000,-000 men, or more than all the adults, male and female, of mankind. If that was so twenty years ago, what is it now? Last century pig iron cost $60 per ton; now it can be produced for $6, and in 1895 the State of Tennessee alone had the furnace capacity to produce a greater quantity of iron than the output of the entire United States in 1860.

Output of the United States, 1885 .... 4,044,000 tons.
Output of the United States, 1895 ....9,446,000 "

This one illustration on iron will answer all Mr. Scott's fallacies on page 28 of the July *Overland*.

To expect relief from the disturbing influences of such enormous increases in production as these facts betoken, such gigantic changes, aggravated in the United States by empirical and selfish legislation and a mania for speculation (all the vast industrial expansion of twenty years past has been accompanied by unexampled speculative inflation, not to say chicanery and fraud, that discounted the future for at least one, if not two, decades), I say, to expect relief from such disturbing influences by a resort to cheap money, a depreciated standard of value,—and extreme protection, —is to trust to antique fallacies which are condemned by history and by the best economic thought of the world.

Now, then, as to Mr. Scott's *tour de force* on protection. He says:

"The Congressional Act of 1894, *throwing wide open the gates to the inflow of foreign cheap labor products*, has operated to close the doors of many American manufactories, turn vast numbers of American workmen into the streets, reduce the price of labor and American products, and to bring gaunt hunger to many an otherwise happy home of the country."

As Mr. Gradgrind would say, "Let us apply a few hard, cold facts" to this heated and groundless rhetorical assertion. The average duty under the several tariffs of the last fifty years has been:

		Average ad valorem rates of duty on dutiable.		Free and dutiable.
Walker	1846–62 inclusive	25.53 per cent		21.55 per cent.
Morrill	1862–73 inclusive	42.86 "		37.29 "
Various	1874–82 inclusive	42.64 "		26.33 "
Acts of 1883	1883–90 inclusive	44.72 "		29.84 "
McKinley	1891–94 inclusive	48.66 "		22.31 "
Wilson, 10 months 1895		41.75 "		20.23 "

The Wilson tariff, an aggregate reduction on free and dutiable goods of only 10 per cent below the McKinley tariff, and on dutiable alone only 1 per cent lower than the average of Republican tariffs for the twenty years from 1862 to 1882, is what Mr. Scott calls ". throwing wide open the gates to the inflow of foreign cheap labor products." Under the McKinley tariff the following shows the workings for first two years, comparatively:

Dutiable goods, 1891 ... $466,455,173
    "   "   1892 ... 355,526,741
             —————————— } Decrease in imports of dutiable goods
             $110,928,432 }   during second year.

Free goods .... 1891 ... $388,064,404
   "   " .... 1892 ... 458,074,604
             —————————— } Increase in imports of free goods
           $ 70,010,200 }   during second year.

Duty collected 1892 as against 1891 decreased $42,-761,431.

The manufactured exports in no year under the McKinley tariff quite touched $184,000,000. In the first year of the Wilson tariff's full operation they exceeded $200,000,000, and they promise in 1896 to amount to $215,000,000. The official figures show that while, for the eight months ending February, 1895, the percentage of exports of manufactured articles to the whole of our exports was 21.26 per cent, for the eight months ending with February last, with a general increase of exports, it rose to 24.41 per cent.

Tariff for other than revenue is a form of class socialism, and inequitable; but even a McKinley tariff, which is a calculable evil, is tolerable compared with the independent, unlimited free coinage of silver by the United States, which would be an incalculable one. I repeat, *a coin is just as bad when debased by over-valuation, if not exchangeable for better, as when unduly alloyed, clipped or sweated.*

In Mr. Scott's article in the July *Overland* he shows
a decided advance in zeal, having progressed from
what he termed in previous papers reprehensible legislation to what he now calls " the crime against silver,"
and remarks that " bimetallism, long tested, proved
highly efficient in performing all the duties required
of money, and therefore may safely be re-established,
and so ought to be." A definition of what Mr. Scott
deems bimetallism now will be in order, and also as to
how he would establish it. I have hitherto quoted the
declaration for gold by the Republicans at St. Louis.
The Democrats at Chicago, in their National Convention, cut the Gordian knot by declaring for the independent, unlimited free coinage of silver by the United
States of America at a ratio of 16 to 1. If Mr. Scott
is at all familiar with the natural laws of money, he
knows that this means silver monometallism for the
United States of America. Prof. Francis A. Walker,
as reported in the press dispatches of the 13th inst., in
a speech at a meeting of the British Bimetallic Society
in London, said :

" It is deeply to be regretted that millions of our
best citizens, as represented at the Chicago Convention
last week, declared for the free coinage of silver at the
ratio of 16 to 1 without waiting for the action of other
countries. This was done passionately, but the effect
will be to maintain the gold standard unimpaired."

The Populist Convention at St. Louis, as reported in
the *Bulletin* of the 24th inst., declares as follows :

" We demand a national currency safe and sound,
issued by the general Government only, a full legal

tender for all debts, private and public, and without the use of banking corporations, a just, equitable and efficient means of distribution direct to the people and through the lawful disbursements of the Government."

Thus it appears that in this campaign the Republicans are for gold; the Democrats are for silver; the Populists are for anything. What is Mr. Scott for? What camp is he in,—Republican or Democratic?

[*From News Letter, August 8, 1896.*]

Editor News Letter :

SIR: I referred in my paper of July 7th (your issue of 11th) to the following remarks of Mr. Scott on page 566 of the *Overland Monthly* for May:

" *That, on a gold basis, money in this country is scarce,* is evidenced by the fact that we, by necessity, issue bonds to the amount of hundreds of millions of dollars, obsequiously paying the bond-takers—mostly foreign—a large premium on the gold received from them."

In addition to the reference therein, I shall oppose to Mr. Scott's erroneous dictum the views of a Republican in good standing, Hon. Thomas B. Reed, who, in a speech at Alfred, Maine, July 28th, said:

" What we want is not more money, but more capital. Money always comes with capital. We have money now, more than we can use, lying idle. We have just exported a lot of it. Money is the transferer of capital, as a hay rake with horse attached is a transferer of hay. More such hay rakes will never make more hay, but more hay will require more such hay rakes and is sure to get them.

" If I sell my house in Portland, or mortgage it for $5,000 and send the result to a Washington State coal mine, and it is spent and comes back to the Casco Bank, my $5,000 worth of capital is in Washington just the same. *What this whole country needs is capital from abroad, from the whole world.* I expect some of you will be surprised and ask whether the world of the United States is not immense and sufficient. Immense, yes; sufficient, no."

For the purpose of external or foreign trade, a debasement of currency is utterly fatuous and pernicious. The coins are estimated at their contents of pure metal, and the international exchange is so rated. The consequence is an apparent rise of foreign prices proportioned to the extent of the debasement. This at once unsettles internal or home trade prices, and they rise to the same level, but with such inequality of motion as may happen to follow from friction, local ignorance, want of communication, or from the intricacies of trade. The inequality of coin-exchange rates which results from this is the broker's opportunity,—margins large enough to cover all commissions and risks; and swiftly and inevitably the good species, or any, bad or good, upon which a differential profit can be made, disappears from circulation. The consequence is that the rising prices which instituted the process are no longer accompanied by an expanding or increasing volume of currency, but, on the contrary, by a decrease in the total of acceptable or efficient currency.

In Great Britain, whose monetary system is on a scientific basis, and the integrity of whose obligations is undoubted, Government revenues for the past year exceeded requirements some forty odd millions of dollars. The trade depression and business stagnation is passing away, as the following information will indicate. The *London Standard*, July 14, 1896, says, relative to bankruptcies :

" The thirteenth annual report by the Board of Trade on the bankruptcies which occurred during the past year has been presented to Parliament. In an introductory report, Sir Courtenay Boyle, after comparing the returns for the past five years, says : ' On the whole it appears to be the fact that the annual amount of trading insolvency, so far at least as private traders and partnerships are concerned, is steadily diminishing, and that it has during the last few years attained a considerably lower level than at any time during the present generation. This is a fact which should not be lost sight of in any review of the position of English commerce. It would be a mistake to treat this fact as bearing conclusively upon the question of the prosperity of trade, but it appears to indicate clearly that, so far as the system of credit is concerned, trade rests on a sound foundation.' "

If there were no agitation for fiat money, if there were no question of the entire integrity of our financial purposes as a people, no question as to the soundness of our monetary status, normal conditions of industry and trade would be restored within twelve months.

I repeat, *that a coin is just as bad when debased by overvaluation, if not exchangeable for better, as when unduly alloyed, clipped or sweated.* What we need is a reformed, not a debased, currency.

[*From News Letter, August 15, 1896.*]

Editor News Letter :

SIR : In my paper of a fortnight ago reference was made to the vast industrial expansion of the past twenty-five years, and its incalculable disturbing influences by reason of its being accompanied by the pernicious growth of artificial trade stimuli, reckless legislation, and a mania for hazardous exploitation to an extent exceeding even its own magnificent proportions. It is impossible to exaggerate the baneful effects of the speculative craze, yet when the evil days have come the remedy clamored for is cheap money, which is but adding insult to injury inflicted upon a deluded people.

It may be of interest to recall past experiences similar in origin, but of less magnitude, because the prodigious industrial development of the present was then undreamed of.

Lord Macaulay says :

" In the earlier part of the reign of William the Third, all the greatest writers on currency were of opinion that a very considerable mass of gold and silver was hidden in secret drawers and behind wainscots.

" The natural effect of this state of things was that a crowd of projectors, ingenious and absurd, visionary and knavish, employed themselves in devising new schemes for the employment of redundant capital. It was about the year 1688 that the word stockjobber was first heard in London. In the short space of four years a crowd of companies, every one of which confidently held out to subscribers the hope of immense gains, sprang into existence,—the insurance company, the paper company, the lute string company, the pearl fishery company, the glass bottle company, the alum company, the Blythe coal company, the swordblade company. There was a tapestry company, which would soon furnish pretty hangings for all the parlors of the middle class, and for all the bedchambers of the higher. There was a copper company, which proposed to explore the mines of England, and held out a hope that they would prove not less valuable than those of Potosi. A company to recover the treasure engulfed with Pharaoh's hosts. There was a diving company, which undertook to bring up precious effects from shipwrecked vessels, and which announced that it had laid in a stock of wonderful machines resembling complete suits of armor. In front of the helmet was a huge glass eye like that of a cyclops, and out of the crest went a pipe through which the air was to be admitted. The whole process was exhibited on the Thames. Fine gentlemen and fine ladies were invited to the show, were hospitably regaled, and were delighted by seeing the divers in their panoply descend into the river and return laden with old iron and ship's tackle. There was a Greenland fishing company, which could not fail to drive the Dutch whalers and herring busses out of the Northern Ocean. There was a tanning company, which promised to furnish leather superior to the best that was brought from Turkey or Russia. There was a society which undertook the office of giving gentlemen liberal education on low terms, and which assumed the sounding name of Royal Academies Company. In a pompous advertisement it was announced that the directors of the Royal Academies Company had engaged the best masters in every branch of knowledge, and were about to issue twenty thousand tickets at twenty shillings each. There was to be a lottery : two thousand prizes were to be drawn, and the fortunate holders of the prizes were to be taught, at the charge of the company, Latin, Greek, Hebrew, French, Spanish, conic sections, trigonometry, heraldry, japanning, fortifications, bookkeeping, and the art of playing the oboe."

All this ended, of course, in a colossal collapse, financial ruin and general misery. Walter Bagehot says:

" The panic was forgotten till Lord Macaulay revived the memory of it. But, in fact, in the South Sea bubble, which has always been remembered, the form was the same, only more extravagant still. The companies in that mania were for objects such as these : ' Wrecks to be fished for on the Irish coast ; insurance of horses and other cattle (two millions) ; insurance of losses by servants ; to make salt water fresh ; for building of hospitals for bastard children ; for building of ships against pirates ; for making of oil from sunflower seeds ; for improving of malt liquors ; for recovery of seamen's wages ; for extracting of silver from lead ; for the transmuting of quicksilver into a malleable and fine metal ; for making of iron with pit coal ; for trading in human hair ; for fatting of hogs ; for a wheel of perpetual motion ; for importing a number of large jackasses from Spain.' But the most strange of all, perhaps, was ' For an undertaking which shall in due time be revealed.' Each subscriber was to pay down two guineas and thereafter receive a share of one hundred, with a disclosure of the unrevealed undertaking ; and, so tempting was the offer, that one thousand of these subscriptions were paid for the same morning, with the proceeds of which the projector decamped the following afternoon."

In 1825 there were speculations in companies nearly as wild, and just before 1866 there were some of a like nature, though not quite so extravagant. The fact is that the owners of savings,—or those who supposed themselves so,—not finding their usual kinds of investment in adequate quantities, rush into anything that holds out specious promises; and, when they find or believe that these tempting investments can be disposed of at a high profit, they rush into them more and more. The first desire is for high interest, but that soon becomes secondary. It is superseded by an appetite for large gains, to be made by selling the principal on which the yield of interest is expected. So long as sales can be effected the mania continues; when they cease to be possible ruin begins.

Ruin has always been the result of such folly, and always will be while time lasts; and sadly enough its evil effects fall, not alone on the unjust and foolish, but on the just and prudent. The list of harebrained, swindling schemes put forth in connection with the South Sea bubble should have made it apparent to the sturdy Britons that there was no need for the importation of large jackasses from Spain or anywhere else. Yet, wild and foolish as the English people were in that and the other instances named, they have been excelled in folly by those of the United States within the past twenty years. And when the chickens come home to roost they are, according to Mr. Scott's logic, to be dispersed by cheap money and more protection. " Angels and ministers of grace defend us!"

Referring to Mr. Bagehot's specification of "an undertaking which shall in due time be revealed," which had for its outcome that the projector went off in the afternoon with the moneys he had collected in the forenoon, it seems very remarkable, and yet is trivial compared to similar schemes that were foisted upon the people of this country,—for example, what was known as the Blind Pool, of some twelve or fourteen years ago, to which millions of dollars were contributed, the disposition of which was left to the caprice of an audacious operator, who invested them in various transportation stocks in order to pool and bull the prices of them. It is a sufficient showing of the madness and iniquity of this and similar deceptions of the times to say that to-day the stocks of this same Blind Pool are not worth fifteen cents on the dollar, and the inflation that was then accomplished had no visible basis except the cupidity and gullibility of the people. The transportation lines are all in the hands of receivers, and the decrease in share values of the companies concerned has been over 85 per cent. And yet the remedy for all the losses, privations and misery resulting from the egregious folly of furthering such schemes is cheap money, itself the most potent of all agencies for the purposes of the gambler and swindler. *I repeat, a coin is just as bad when debased by overvaluation, if not exchangeable for better, as when unduly alloyed, clipped or sweated.*

Speculation run riot through the land,—particularly in building railroads (and even towns) that were not needed,—and what took place at Vancouver, Seattle,

Tacoma, Winnipeg, Sioux City, Omaha, Kansas City, Denver, Wichita, Los Angeles, San Diego, and scores of other places, is illustrated by the fate of a sister city. The loot of a Northwestern city, as told in a San Francisco daily of December 16, 1895, is another and a yet more startling revelation of such folly, and its entail of crime and financial ruin. A public debt of $5,000,000 now hangs over that city of only 25,000 people, with interest on the debt at $1,000 a day, and an assessed property valuation of only $26,000,000. For the $5,000,000 of city obligations, it has probably not to exceed $1,000,000 of property and $4,000,000 of debt, with nothing to show for the latter, and all this out of a vain and knavish endeavor to evolve something out of nothing, for which the panacea now is,—cheap money.

Our financial and industrial crises have, as hitherto shown, usually followed periods of marked activity, but have been owing to or influenced by various causes,—vicious financial legislation; extreme protection, so called; wastefulness, governmental, corporative and personal; undue expansion of credit; wildcat schemes of speculation; corporate ventures capitalized into stock. shares beyond all reason, beyond any just proportion to the money actually invested; mushroom towns with plush hotels and nickel-plated paraphernalia generally, etc., all accompanied by endless assertion of self-sufficiency. And now the last and biggest bubble of all is " free silver," the inevitable effect of which would be to rob all wage-earners. The reformation of all these evils requires more virtue than ever was or ever can be found in money, fiat or otherwise. If the gentlemen who are advocating silver in the magazines of California would consider the speculation that the American public has indulged in for thirty years in swindling projects of every name and nature, and stock shares endlessly inflated, it seems to me that they would doubt the power of Government to obviate the evil consequences of such enormous waste, moral as well as material, by more " protection " and the issue of fiat money, whether metal or paper.

> " Transgression brings retributive stings
> To candle-makers as well as kings."

There is no real capital except what comes from previous labor performed; and a government is as powerless to bring wealth into existence out of nothing by fiat as an individual. If it be ascertained that such a device is practical, it is in truth the discovery of the philosopher's stone, and more's the pity it was not discovered sooner.

John Law conceived the idea of making all the property of France security for the money that country issued. As the historian Blanqui ironically remarks, " What could be a finer mortgage than France." Yet, says Blanqui, when the financial debauch was over: " Of all the industrial values produced under the hot atmosphere of Law's system, nothing remained but bankruptcy, ruin and desolation. Landed property alone had not perished in the tempest." One of its lessons is that neither real estate nor anything else not immediately convertible into real money, money of intrinsic equivalency, can support a circulating currency. Yet the lesson was unheeded even by France, and during the Revolution alleged statesmen came forward in overwhelming numbers to insist that John Law's money had at first restored prosperity, that the immeasurable wretchedness and wrong it finally caused had resulted from overissue, and that such an over-issue was possible only under a despotism. The collossal ruin that was wrought by the issue of assignats is a matter of word-wide notoriety.

Professor Perry, in his "Elements of Political Economy," says of the crazy monetary schemes of the French Revolution:

"The distress and consternation into which a country falls when its current measure of services is disturbed and destroyed is past all powers of description. The prisons and the guillotine did not compare with the assignats in causing suffering during those six years. This example is significant because it shows the powerlessness of even the strongest and most unscrupulous government to regulate the value of anything. The assignats were depreciating during the very months in which Robespierre and the Committee of Public Safety were wielding the power of life and death in France with terrific energy. They did their utmost to stop the sinking of the revolutionary paper. But value knows its own laws, and follows them in spite of decrees and penalties."

The history of the world is replete with examples of nations that have thought to get over hard times and become suddenly rich by depreciating their currency. The wrecks from this source line the pages of history. Not one has ever succeeded, and not one ever will succeed, in bettering its condition by depreciating its money standard. Our people must learn this important truth, and the sooner they do so the better it will be for their welfare. I take the liberty of quoting the language of a San Francisco writer of the present, in which he characterizes the "perverse spirit of the times, as everywhere manifesting itself in wild aspirations for impossible advantages, in the resurrection of the discredited beliefs and methods of antiquity,—in cutting loose from all that is conservative,—in a reign of unreason." In quest of what?

I repeat that honesty, patience, hard work and frugality are the only remedies for the ills we have largely drawn upon our own shoulders, and which we must bear until relieved by common-sense methods of our own devising.

[From News Letter, August 22, 1896.]

Editor News Letter:

SIR: In the July *Overland* Mr. Scott says:

" In the United States, gold and silver on an equal footing and at an established parity were employed as legal money, with happy effect, from 1792 to 1873. During this period of eighty-one years, their value lines were nearly coincident, *and doubtless would have so continued till the present time but for the demonetizing crime of silver in 1873.* * * *

" Gold monometallism has proved highly fluctuating —appreciated over 100 per cent in twenty-three years— and should therefore be permanently abolished. Bimetallism, long tested, proved highly efficient in performing all the duties required of money, and therefore may safely be re-established, and ought so to be."

These assertions are not in accord with the facts of history. Bimetallism is impossible in the United States under the independent, unlimited free coinage of silver as legal tender at a ratio of 16 to 1, or, for that matter, at any other ratio. Prof. Francis A. Walker, the ablest bimetallist in the United States, says in the preface to his recently published work, " International Bimetallism :"

"Though a bimetallist of the international type to the very center of my being, I have ever considered the efforts made by this country, for itself alone, to rehabilitate silver, as prejudicial equally to our own national interests and to the cause of true international bimetallism. For us to throw ourselves alone into the breach, simply because we think silver ought not to have been demonetized and ought now to be restored, would be a piece of quixotism unworthy the sound practical sense of our people."

Referring to Mr. Scott's observations on due proportions of gold and silver, I would remark, the "due proportion " which Mr. Hamilton and Mr. Jefferson considered and discussed in connection with coinage was the average of coinage ratios in European countries. The commodity ratios were then between 15 and 16 to 1. At a coinage ratio of 15½ to 1, gold disappeared; at 16 to 1, silver disappeared; now the commodity ratio is 31 to 1, and of course, under the free coinage of silver at 16 to 1, all gold would instantly disappear from current circulation. The concurrence of the commercial world fixes mercantile ratios, and the United States, immense as it is, cannot change them by free coinage. *I repeat, that a coin is just as bad when debased by overvaluation, if not exchangeable for better, as when unduly alloyed, clipped or sweated.*

General Weaver, in his speech at St. Louis presenting Hon. W. J. Bryan for the Populist nomination, stated that the issue was between the gold standard, gold bonds and bank currency on the one hand, and the bimetallic standard, no bonds and a Government currency on the other, asserting that the conflict can neither be postponed nor avoided. Now this statement, divested of all sophistry, resolves itself into this: A gold standard of value, with silver as auxiliary, and a currency redeemable in money of intrinsic equivalency upon one side, and upon the other Government fiat money. That is just what it means in the end, and there need be no doubt about it.

I had the opportunity of talking with a leading California Populist, and asked him if it was the belief of the people whom he represented that the par of the metals could be maintained under independent, unlimited free coinage on a ratio of 16 parts of silver to 1 of gold, and he frankly derided the possibility of such a thing, and declared that the Populists advocated the independent, unlimited free coinage of silver as a means of discharging debts with cheap money, and that, if silver money did not prove cheap enough, they would, if intrusted with power, resort to fiat paper money.

Whether the gentlemen who cast the majority vote for free silver at the Chicago Convention will make so frank an admission I do not know, but Governor Altgeld and others are reported as clearly defining the contest to be what Henry George phrased one of the " House of Want " against the " House of Have."

In discussing money the advocates of the independent, unlimited free coinage of silver universally ignore the natural laws of money (which are certain to control finally), and generally display, not only a misapprehension of the essential principles of money, that, in view of the all-important nature of the subject, is simply astounding, but also a lamentable unfamiliarity with its technical and legal status.

In a speech of the present Democratic candidate for President, Hon. W. J. Bryan, delivered before the Trans-Mississippi Congress in St. Louis, he declared that "true bimetallism means that the value of a dollar shall be regulated, not by artificial laws, but by the natural laws of supply and demand," and then immediately proceeds to controvert his own position by saying that the coinage ratio shall be 16 to 1, when the commercial ratio is about 31 to 1. The natural law is that coins shall be equivalent to that for which they are accepted,—go where they will. The imposition of a forced ratio and legal-tender quality is a purely arbitrary and artificial arrangement, and sets in motion the Gresham Law. Senator Turpie, as chairman of a silver convention in Indiana, some time ago, declared that the gold coinage of the country was fiat to the extent of 10 per cent, and predicated his entire speech upon this erroneous assumption. Quite recently Governor Matthews of Indiana declared that we should not make gold the standard, while gold has specifically been the standard for twenty-three years and by custom and mercantile concurrence for sixty years. These examples are rivaled by silver advocates in California, who set at defiance the facts of history and teachings of economic science in their insistence on empiricism pure and simple,—an empiricism, too, that has encountered countless practical illustrations of its own futility ; and Layman is constrained to say that Mr. Scott is no exception to the rule; that when he essayed to discuss money he selected a subject with which—its laws, history and modern functions—he is manifestly not familiar.

In the February *Overland* Mr. Scott says:

" Not only have the demonetizing acts with respect to silver reduced the world's redemption money fully fifty per cent, but *they have palsied its powers of recuperation, have effected a scarcity of money, and thereby infested our country's doors with countless packs of ravenous wolves.*"

And in the July *Overland* he says:

" Mr. John Sherman, largely responsible for the evils that have been wrecking the country for the last twenty years and upward, pleads guilty to the charge of participancy in the crime against silver,—against the people in 1873,—sets forth the truths as to the effects of that crime, and for his execrable part therein offers ignorance as his apology, than which, except fraud, it would be hard to find anything more humiliating."

We might expect such utterances from Mr. Coxey, Mr. Debs, Governor Altgeld, Senator Tillman or Professor Andrews, but not from a would-be leader of the Republican party of California. However, greenback and silver legislation is chiefly responsible for the cloud of doubt that hangs over our financial status, that depresses industry and retards the return of prosperity. When confidence prevails, the activity of exchange is at once manifest, money moves about rapidly, is handled everywhere, and seems the more abundant because of its general distribution; but *when political commotion, " false doctrines, heresy and schism " create alarm, capital halts, money moves slowly, is frequently*

hoarded, and complaints are unjustly made of its absence.
It is the persistency of the fiat movement that causes
capital to withdraw from investment and hold aloof
from new enterprises,—hence the continued stagnation
and depression of business in the United States.

The following is from the May *Overland :*

" The Congressional Act of 1894, *throwing wide open
the gates to the inflow of foreign cheap labor products
has operated to close the doors of many American
manufactories, turn vast numbers of American workmen into the streets, reduce the price of labor and
American products, and to bring gaunt hunger to
many an otherwise happy home of the country."*

Confronted by the historical lessons cited in this
series of papers, and familiar to all well-informed men,
Mr. Scott must perceive the unwisdom of such rhetorical flourishes ; the uninformed may take them for
facts, and thereby cause the rapid pace at which the
country is already moving toward a perverted socialism
to be further accelerated.

On page 565 of the May *Overland* Mr. Scott says :

" Monometallists seem to regard gold as supernal,
divine. The cathode rays of their minds photograph
gold only. The disposition which Moses, the divinely
appointed agent for promulgating the commands of the
Great Author of the Decalogue, made of the golden
calf set up in the wilderness, evidences his estimate
with respect to the divinity of gold. Permit me
respectfully to suggest that Layman well con this
cogent lesson of the great Law Giver."

Layman begs to assure Mr. Scott that he cares no
more for gold than for iron or coal, but considers the
subject from a purely historical and economical standpoint. However, as it is alleged that Mr. Scott is now

a Presidential elector for the Republican party (the party that committed "the crime against silver") and *on the present gold standard*, it seems in order to ask him if he is disposed to con the cogent lessons of the great Law Giver for himself, and with a mind receptive of wise precept. On the presumption that he is, the following is submitted to his consideration:

"Ye shall do no unrighteousness in judgment, in meteyard, in weight or in measure. Just balances, just weights, a just ephah, and a just hin, shall ye have."

Leviticus xix: 35, 36.

Without attempting to recapitulate Mr. Scott's contention in detail, suffice it to say it amounts to this, viz, that scarcity of money and nonprotection of home industries are the causes of the evils which now afflict the body politic and social; and, if I have interpreted him aright, that more money—free silver—and higher tariff legislation would remedy them.

To summarize my position in this discussion I affirm that, in general, what the country needs is at least a rest from tariff tinkering and a reformed, not a debased, currency, with more common sense, honesty, patience, industry and frugality, and maintain as follows:

First—I recognize the peculiar hardships of the American wheat farmer, but they are largely because of competition with Argentina peons, Indian ryots and Russian peasants, still further aggravated by the reduced value of horses, mules, oats, hay, etc., owing to steam and electric power on street railways, and the use of bicycles. But in California the farmer's obligations are payable in gold, and the unlimited free coinage of silver by the United States, which would inevitably drive gold out of current circulation, could not remedy but would aggravate his misfortunes, and further would probably bring farm laborers to the same plight as their foreign competitors.

Second—That the welfare of the whole mass of mankind is finally promoted by obtaining cheaply all the necessaries of life, if it can be shown that alongside of these lower prices for life's necessaries wages have in the main increased, *and they have.*

Third—That prices of commodities move in obedience to natural and inherent causes, independent of circulating money quantities. The economic phenomena of the past fifty years demonstrates this.

Fourth—That gold and silver coins never have in any country circulated simultaneously, concurrently and indiscriminately, as legal tender, at a fixed ratio under unrestricted free coinage of both metals.

Fifth—That the international bimetallic theory—the quantitative or so-called double-standard pool theory—lacks foundation in any known principle of economic law, and is a fallacy, rejected as such by most modern economists and financiers of credit and renown, and by every Western power of any commercial importance whatsoever.

Sixth—That by natural law there is but one way to provide for bimetallism in any country, and that is to make the more precious metal the standard, and then float such an amount of the cheaper metal as can be kept upon an undoubted equality through interchangeability.

Seventh—That there can be no such thing as a double standard. We must have either gold or silver for our standard.

Eighth—That Government cannot create values, and that the current value of moneys is determined independently of the decree of kings, legislative enactments, or Government fiat.

Ninth—That a coin is just as bad when debased by overvaluation, if not exchangeable for better, as when unduly alloyed, clipped or sweated.

Tenth—That there never was a contrivance so potent for injuring the masses of mankind as so-called cheap money.

Eleventh—That there is not a free-coinage country in the world to-day that is not on a silver basis.

Twelfth—That there is not a gold-standard country in the world to-day that does not use silver as money along with gold.

Thirteenth—That there is not a silver-standard country in the world to-day that uses any gold as money along with silver.

Fourteenth—That there is not a silver-standard country in the world to-day that has more than one-third as much money in circulation per capita as the United States has.

Fifteenth—That there is not a silver-standard country in the world to-day where the laboring man receives as fair pay for his day's work as he now does in the United States under the present gold standard.

I repeat: There can be no such thing as a double-standard. We must have either gold or silver for our standard.

UNDER WHICH KING, BEZONIAN?

A Layman begs permission to say a few words more. In the May *Overland*, page 566, we find:

" It is to be apprehended that the reader will perceive that Layman's comments are hypercritical, evincing an aim to say something brilliantly carping rather than to present truth. The writer would respectfully ' commend him to a prudent husbandry of his resources.' "

As a measure of relief to Mr. Scott's solicitude in advising Layman to " husband his resources," Layman answers that from the force of habit, as well as a due regard for the friendly admonition, he has carefully held in reserve sundry pages of·manuscript on the subject of money in general, and silver in particular, which can be drawn upon in case of future need.

On page 568, same number of the magazine, he observes :

" Charity suggests that Layman may be ' mad.' If he be so, it would, in view of his utterances as to the power of Government to create value by statutory enactment, seem the acme of hyperbole to say, ' Much learning doth make thee mad.' "

Now, in view of the stubborn facts of history, past and present, does Mr. Scott think his " Hard Times " articles entitle *him* to distinction for " much learning?" A Layman cannot perceive that his expositions are edifying, nor refrain from characterizing his statistics as inaccurate, his assertions as erroneous, his inferences as fallacious, and his conclusions as lame and impotent; wherefore he pronounces them unsatisfactory. Let him be assured that A Layman has not been moved by any desire to say something " brilliantly carping," but, considering the momentous issues before the people, is sincerely regretful that a gentleman of Mr. Scott's standing should have gone so far astray in his monetary vagaries and Populistic views as he has, for it is calculated to make the judicious grieve. " Money is not a question of politics or sentiment, but of science and ethics. It comes without being called and goes without being arrested, is deaf to advances and insensible to threats."

When Paul stood before King Agrippa at Cæsarea, discoursing of righteousness and judgment to come,—things the haughty Festus, who was present, did not understand,—and defended himself against unjust accusations, the disdainful remark of the latter was fitly answered, " *I am not mad, most noble Festus, but speak forth the words of truth and soberness.*"

A LAYMAN.

P. S.—Since the foregoing was written, Mr. Scott is reported, in the *Examiner* of the 12th inst., as having spoken before a Republican meeting at Santa Rosa, and in part his remarks were summarized as follows :

" He controverted the statements that hard times had followed the so-called demonetization of silver, claiming that the period since that alleged act had been one of unexampled prosperity. He declared that the claim made by the silver men that the restoration of free coinage would result in the raising of prices of products and labor is fallacious."

A Layman is pleased to observe these evidences of conversion, but is unable to perceive how Mr. Scott can reconcile them with his four articles on " Hard Times " in the *Overland Monthly* of this year, except upon the assumption that a great light has shone upon him.

[*From News Letter, September 5, 1896.*]

Editor News Letter:

SIR: Recurring to the subject of the independent, unlimited free coinage of silver by the United States, the question has been simplified by the action of the Chicago Convention in its declarations and nominations. The independent, unlimited free coinage of silver by the United States means silver monometallism; in other words, a silver basis only for the money currency of this country.

The most recent expressions of such men as Moreton, Frewen and Dr. Ahrendt ("clouds they are without water, carried about of winds; trees whose fruit withereth, without fruit"), in the readiness they show to have the United States throw itself into the gulf of national bimetallism—that is, the independent, unlimited free coinage of silver—remind me of the patriotic attitude of Artemus Ward during our Civil War, when he declared himself willing to sustain the war so long as there were any of his wife's relatives left to send to the front.

As to what the status would be under independent, unlimited free coinage of silver by this country, I have repeatedly referred to that in previous articles, and as to the present attitude of Mr. Frewen, Dr. Ahrendt and others, who claim that the United States can safely undertake such a step, I herewith oppose thereto the most recent expressions of Prof. Francis A. Walker, by odds the ablest bimetallist in the United States, and second to none in the world:

"Though a bimetallist of the international type to the very center of my being, I have ever considered the efforts made by this country, for itself alone, to rehabilitate silver, as prejudicial equally to our own national interests and to the cause of true international bimetallism. For us to throw ourselves alone into the breach simply because we think silver ought not to have been demonetized and ought now to be restored, would be a piece of quixotism unworthy the sound practical sense of our people."

Prof. Walker further says, under the head of "Silver Coinage in the United States:"

"The United States had continued the mischievous policy of coining silver at the ratio of 16 to 1, which had been begun under the Act of February 28, 1878, while the agitation of the subject throughout the country became more and more intense. As the views and wishes of those who have not failed since 1876 to press upon the public mind and upon the attention of Congress the importance of action to restore silver to its former rank as a money metal have differed very widely, it seems right to say a few words in characterization of the classes of persons in the United States who have been wont to call themselves bimetallists. We have, first, the inhabitants of the silver-producing States. These citizens have what is called a particular interest, as distinct from a participation in the general interest. The restoration of silver to the position, as a money metal, which it occupied down to 1873, would, at any time during the past fifteen years, have meant to these people a higher price for the products of their community or section, perhaps of their individual properties. Their interest in the maintenance of silver as a money metal has been of the same nature as the interest of Pennsylvanians in the duties on pig iron, and of the citizens of Ohio and Michigan in the duties on wool.

Silver coinage is with them not a financial but an industrial issue. Although the silver-mining industry of the country is not large, in comparison with scores and scores of others, it has yet been able to exert a high degree of power in our politics, partly because of our system of equal representation in the Senate, partly because of the eagerness and intensity with which the object has been pursued. The second consists of those who, without any particular interest in the production of silver, are yet, in their general economic views, in favor of superabundant and cheap money. Among the leaders of this element have been found the very men who, between 1868 and 1876, were foremost in advocating the greenback heresy. Beaten on the issue of greenback inflation, they have taken up the issue of silver inflation. They have adopted the cause of silver, not because silver is more valuable than irredeemable paper (which they prefer), but because it is, and more especially because it promises still further to become, cheaper than gold at the legal ratio. They are for depreciated silver because, in their view, it is the next best thing (by which they mean what we should call the next worst thing) to greenbacks. Those who constitute the element now under consideration are not true bimetallists. What they really want is silver inflation.

" I would not wish to be understood as refusing to regard as real bimetallists many persons who, in the situation existing, are in favor of the free coinage of silver. The test of the true bimetallist is simply this: Is it his object to secure an absolute or approximate par-of-exchange between the two metals, and to promote the fullest use of both as money which may be consistent with the working of the laws of trade? If this is his bona fide wish and purpose, any man is entitled to be considered a bimetallist, even though he may propose a mistaken policy in any given place and time. The error of those free-coinage men who are also sincerely in favor of the larger bimetallism is in failing to recognize: (1) that the time has passed when even France herself could maintain the function she performed from 1803 to 1873, so greatly have the stocks of the precious metals been increased, so vast is now the mass of securities immediately marketable, so much more rapid is the communication of news and the transportation of specie, so potent has been the influence of Germany through its passing over from the silver to the gold states, so much have trade and production developed with the improvement of arts and the increase of population; (2) that the people of the United States normally use vastly less metal money than the French now do, or than the French did in the early time, and, by consequence, this country is not, and has never been, in a position to exert an equal effect upon the market for the money metals.

"In 1889 and 1890 the agitation for the free coinage of silver had risen to such a height as to threaten the inauguration of a system which would, in the opinion of all conservative men, not only monometallists but bimetallists, have speedily brought the United States to silver monometallism, having a par-of-exchange with the East and with the states of South America, but with a large and fluctuating premium upon gold. More than once this result appears to have been averted only by the aggressive courage and stubborn persistency of a few members of the House of Representatives. The Senate at this time, owing largely to the system of equal representation of States, could have furnished no barrier to such a movement; and there was great doubt whether President Harrison would interpose the executive veto. Under these circumstances, with the plea that it was necessary to concede something in order to avert free coinage, was passed the so-called Sherman bill of 1890, which provided for the purchase by the Treasury of 4,500,000 ounces of silver per month. This measure was of a thoroughly mischievous character and effect. That it was necessary to make this concession to the free-coinage party, I, for one, do not believe. I am so little of a doctrinaire that I should hesitate to say that, in all matters political, flat and contemptuous resistance to unreasonable demands and evil measures is always a safe policy; but my study of financial history creates an increasing conviction that the only good policy in dealing with financial crazes is to fight them, without asking or giving quarter. The men of 1890, to whom the people had entrusted their powers of legislation, did not deal with the matter in this spirit. Doubtless politics, in the lowest sense of the word, entered not a little to affect their temper, and the coming presidential election cast its baleful shadow before."

Leaving out of account all else, we will now proceed to the consideration of how the independent, unlimited free coinage of silver would affect the wage-earners of this country, of whom I am one. The history of civilization, and particularly of the past six hundred years, shows conclusively the impossibility of maintaining a parity between gold and silver at fixed ratios as legal-tender money under unlimited free coinage; and the question that confronts the working people of whatsoever kind or character in this country is, What would be the purchasing power of silver-standard money, under the independent, unlimited free coinage of silver, as compared with that under the present gold-standard money, under limited Goverment coinage of silver and the gold par maintained by Government? A silver dollar has now, as since 1878, a purchasing power of one hundred cents.

Mr. Mattias Romero, Minister of Mexico to the United States, said, in an article in the *North American Review*, June, 1895:

"It is rather puzzling and bewildering to some travelers who go from this country to Mexico to see that a United States silver dollar containing less silver bullion than a Mexican silver dollar was exchanged there for two Mexican silver dollars, when pure silver was at about fifty-nine cents an ounce; but in such an exchange the Mexican silver dollar is sold for the price of the bullion it contains, while the United States silver dollar is the representative of a gold dollar, and is therefore merchandise bought to pay debts in the United States or Europe."

Under the independent, unlimited free coinage of silver, the purchasing power of a silver dollar—or any sign or instrumentality of a silver dollar—would be precisely the bullion or commodity value of the metal composing it, and no more. A Mexican silver dollar, with six grains more silver than our standard silver dollar, is worth now in San Francisco just 53 cents; and the expectation that Government fiat would make a United States free silver dollar good for a purchasing power of one hundred cents when worth only fifty odd cents would simply be disappointed, and the holder would find himself subjected to a discount in the way of increased prices for all rents paid and necessaries purchased. *Would each and every such holder have power under such circumstances to compel his employer to raise his wages correspondingly? If so, the present differs from all former times.*

If the laboring men of this country wanted to sell silver, or were now being paid in silver *on a free-coinage basis*, there might be some sense in it. But the laboring men of this country are practically getting paid in gold, not silver. What good will it do a man who doesn't own silver, who doesn't sell silver, who now gets paid in gold values, to be paid in silver?

But there is another way to look at it. Gold means high wages to the laborer. It is so in all gold-using countries. Recently, Mr. Cannon, a free silver delegate in Congress from Utah, alleged first, that prices of goods were low here because they were measured in gold, and then that, on account of wages here being paid in gold,—which was costly,—and wages in India, China and Japan being paid in silver,—which was worth only one-half what it had been,—they had fifty per cent advantage, and that therefore there was danger of our manufactures being driven from the world's markets: which means their wages are so much lower than ours, on account of the gold standard here, that, unless our wages are reduced to theirs,—unless prices are inflated here in this country so that our gold wages will buy no more than their silver wages,—their labor will tend to drive out ours. In other words, the free silver propaganda, however intended, is practically a proposition to cut the wages of the laborers of this country in half.

Sir Henry Meysey Thompson is one of the leading silver advocates of England. He offered a prize for the best essay explaining how it was that China and India and other silver-using countries were getting an advantage over England, and a great many people competed for that prize. Mr. Jamieson, the British Consul at Shanghai, wrote so good a paper that he was awarded the prize. He says :

" Wages in the gold-using countries have, through the appreciation of gold, become 100 per cent dearer than they were relatively to silver wages; and the manufacturer in the silver-standard countries can obtain his labor at half the cost which he formerly paid,"

and gives the natural result thereof in these words : " while old-established industries in England are barely paying expenses, new industries in India are arising and paying handsomely." *The change proposed by silver advocates in England is to evade these gold wages and raise prices of goods so that* the British workman, though getting the same nominal wages in silver, will really get only half the actual wages he gets now, and the British manufacturer may thus be enabled to compete with the Indian manufacturer.

A somewhat similar view is taken by Señor Romero, the Mexican Minister at Washington, in his *North American Review* article already mentioned, when he asserts that the depreciation of silver has favored Mexican capitalists by lowering the actual wages of their employees. *There is the silver question in a nutshell.*

As to the wage-earners, it is simply a question as to whether they are getting too high wages. They may as well face the question. If wage-earners believe they are getting too high wages, and that this country is suffering in consequence, all they have to do is to accept lower wages; or, if they prefer a roundabout way, they can favor the independent, unlimited free coinage of silver, and practically they will get their wages cut down one-half without any further trouble on their part.

The earnings from wages in this country approximate 7,200 million dollars per annum, and the scaling of the purchasing power of the mouey received for them is a question that every worker must consider. Let each then, in sober, serious earnest, ask himself or herself, How would it affect me? I can see no reason, not even the shadow of a reason, why my fellow-workmen the land over—be they managers, agents, clerks, porters or laborers of whatever kind—should deem it beneficial to be paid their wages in silver, really worth, under unlimited free coinage, only fifty odd cents to the dollar, and blindly trust to the fiat of the Government for its (*i. e.*, the silver) having had the purchasing power of one hundred cents to the dollar conferred upon it. That were a thing that has never been achieved in any period of human history. I repeat, let each one ask himself or herself this question, How would it affect me? Let every wage-earner consider these facts now while he has the option.

One of the most pertinent answers put forth to the claim of the silver advocates that the policy of independent, unlimited free coinage would be of benefit to the working people is the testimony of the Mayor of El Paso, Texas, whose position on the border line certainly enables him to know the absolute truth of the matters he alleges, while, at the same time, it constitutes no presumptive evidence that he is actuated by a desire to furnish aid and comfort to the "goldbugs." Here it is, just as he wrote it out in answer to an inquiring correspondent:

"I, R. F. Campbell, Mayor of the City of El Paso, Texas, hereby certify that I have made a careful and diligent inquiry into the wholesale price of some common articles of merchandise in the City of El Paso, Texas, and in the City of Juarez, Mexico, just across the Rio Grande, and at this date, August 7, 1896, the prices of the following articles in the two cities are as follows, those on this side of the river being reckoned in United States money and those on the other side in Mexican silver:

	In United States.	In Mexico.
Breakfast bacon, per pound	$ .11½	$ .32
Ham, per pound	.11½	.32
Matches, per gross	.60	1.20
Pickles, in five-gallon kegs	2.25	6.50
Vinegar, in five-gallon kegs	.60	1.40
Baking soda, per dozen	1.06	2.40
Salt, in two-pound sacks	.40	.90
Macaroni, per pound	.10	.25
Royal baking powder	4.00	9.00
Molasses, per gallon	.75	1.69
Beans, per pound	.03	.17
Cheese, per pound	.12½	.20
Candles, per box	5.00	11.75
Catsup, per dozen	2.00	6.25
Jelly, per dozen	2.00	5.00
Dried plums, per pound	.11	.25
Dried apples and peaches, per pound	.11	.25
Dried prunes, per pound	.10	.20

	In United States.	In Mexico.
Cornstarch, per dozen	$1.06	$1.90
Lemon extract, per dozen	1.00	1.90
Vanilla extract, per dozen	2.25	3.00
Arbuckle's coffee, per pound	.20	.40
Soap, per box	3.75	5.00
Tea, per pound	.35 to 1.00	.70 to 1.50
Deviled ham, per dozen	2.90	6.50
Sugar, per sack of 100 pounds	5.50	10.75
Flour, per sack of 100 pounds	2.25	6.50
Rice, per pound	.05	.11
Condensed milk, per case	8.00	21.50
Canned tomatoes, per case	2.25	7.90
Canned peas, per case	2.40	8.50
Crackers, per pound	.07½	.21½

" The Mexican prices are the prices which prevail in the free zone, on which there is a small duty. Of course, in the interior they would be much higher. I also find and do hereby certify that Mexican labor in Mexico in the larger cities is paid 75 cents to $1.50 per day in Mexican silver. The highest price for the very best and most skilled labor is $2 per day in the same kind of money. In the interior of Mexico, in the country and smaller cities, the wages paid are from twenty per cent to thirty per cent lower than that given above.

"Given under my hand and seal of office on this seventh day of August, A. D. 1896.

"R. F. CAMPBELL,

"Mayor of El Paso, Texas."

We have been especially treating of wage-earners. Let us now consider savings bank depositors (largely composed of that class) in the single State of California. The records show as follows:

1870—depositors, 47,535; deposits, $ 36,555,909

1896— " 169,856; " 132,422,351

Here is an increase in dollars of 266 per cent and an increase in the number of depositors of 261 per cent in twenty-five years. This State is the richest per capita of any in the Union—in round figures, $2,100 per head. Let these 169,856 industrious, prudent, frugal wage-earners ask themselves if their interest will be promoted by the independent, unlimited free coinage of silver.

The foregoing furnishes object lessons that every wage-earner, particularly every voter, should study, with a view to the proper determination of the question upon the basis of "enlightened self-interest."

I am a Democrat of the straightest sect of Jefferson, Jackson, Benton, Tilden and Cleveland, and I insist that *a coin is just as bad when debased by overvaluation, if not exchangeable for better, as when unduly alloyed, clipped or sweated.*

[*From News Letter, October 3, 1896.*]

Editor News Letter :

Sir : An excursion I made to the Northwest in the past two weeks prevented me from complying with your request for further contributions on the subject of silver and hard times. During my absence I had the opportunity of reading the remarks of the Hon. Francis G. Newlands, M. C., of Nevada, in April and May last before the Congressional Committee on Ways and Means, on the subject of Japanese competition,—the effect of the competition of silver-standard countries upon our agricultural and manufacturing industries, the remedy, etc.; and in the columns of the city press

of September 17th I find an extract, at least, from
Mr. Newlands' address of the 16th in this city, as to
the prosperity that would follow the independent, unlimited free coinage of silver by the United States,
wherein, amongst other things, he says:

" I maintain that the free coinage of silver at the rate
of 16 to 1 by this country is practicable; *that it will
restore the old relative value of silver and gold*, release
this country from its dependence on foreign countries,
impair the efficiency of the cheap labor of silver-standard
countries in competition with our own, restore the value
of our agricultural products with which we pay our
debts abroad, and save this country from a manufacturing competition that will prove destructive."

Appreciating Mr. Newlands' courtesy in providing
me with a copy of his remarks before the Committee,
containing altogether some sixty-five pages of closely
printed matter, I take pleasure in testifying to the
graceful diction which characterizes his verbal as well
as printed observations. In view, however, of his
admitted talents, I am the more astonished that he
should be chasing rainbows in his advocacy of the
independent, unlimited free coinage of silver by the
United States, which, subjected to analysis, are even
less tangible than the fascinating but elusive displays
that accompany summer showers.

Mr. Newlands' contention may be compressed into
two points, namely: (1) an agreement with the silver-
standard or debtor nations for the greater use of silver;
or (2) its independent, unlimited free coinage by the
United States, with the alleged object of increasing its
value so as to raise the price of labor in silver-standard

countries, and thereby, to such extent as wage rates there might be raised, mitigate the competition of the labor of those countries with that of the United States of America.

In the discussion of this subject by the best informed writers and advocates of international bimetallism, the conclusion has been reached that, without reference to the local rate of wages paid in different countries, it is a fact that wages paid in gold are doubly as valuable in purchasing power as wages paid in silver, and that the result of the unlimited free coinage of silver, so far as competing silver-standard countries go, would be to reduce wages on a gold basis to an equality with silver wages, or to raise prices on a silver standard until they overcame the difference. Now in either case the result is a direct blow to labor in gold-using countries, and if we admit, for the sake of argument, that in the matter of farm products, for example, wheat and cotton,—but practically these, and these only,—the farmer might possibly derive some advantage, it must be remembered that numerically the farmers represent considerably less than 30 per cent of the working element of the United States. In other words, there are over 20,000,000 workers in the United States and less than 6,000,000 farmers.

To return now to Mr. Newlands' first proposition— and, by the way, his San Francisco speech of the 16th, reprinted the 27th, is but a brief synopsis of his remarks before the Congressional Committee—to return, I say, to his first proposition, which is to form a monetary alliance with debtor countries: He lays especial emphasis upon Russia, calling attention to the fact that Russia has a numerous population, say, all told, 120,000,000, and therefore, upon his theory, great power to "*absorb money;*" but he should have borne in mind that the greater proportion of this population is composed of nomadic hordes, not at all a commercial people in the modern sense. Why not consider the present and past relations of copper "cash" to silver taels in China? Moreover, the quantity of metallic money that can be put into actual circulation is limited. We have "absorbed" over six hundred millions of silver money in the past twenty years, and over one-half of it—three hundred and fifty millions of dollars—has no more monetary efficiency than so much stored copper matte, bar lead or pig iron. Regarding Russia, however, from his financial standpoint, as numerically potential, he dwells upon its power of "*absorbing money,*" without appearing to take into consideration the essential fact that the basic function of money is to serve as a medium or vehicle of exchange, and that in the great commerce of the world it is not a thing *for* which commodities are exchanged, but the means *whereby* they are exchanged. In short, as has been aptly said, "*Men do not work for money, but for money's worth;*" and Mr. Newlands was forced to admit on page 12 of his statement before the Congressional Committee that there is no other advantage in a free-silver currency than to diminish the cost of labor, while in another part of his remarks his argument is that the free coinage of silver would raise its value to that of gold. His San Francisco speech bears the latter interpretation; yet on pages 12 and 18 of his more deliberate

statement he practically admits that the effect would be
to reduce wages by the introduction of a cheaper money.
Again referring to his theory of a country " *absorbing
money*," and the emphasis with which he dwells upon
Russia as a favorable country for that experiment with
silver, he is doubtless familiar with the proceedings of
the International Convention at Brussels in 1892.   If
so, he will remember that the representatives of Russia
were just as positive in regard to the impracticability
of bimetallism under unlimited free coinage, that is,
the concurrent circulation of both metals as legal-tender
money, as the representatives of England, France or
Germany; and the representatives of these three countries asserted, without qualification, that the possibility
of a free-coinage bimetallism was out of the question,
and that the case was closed, as did those of Austria,
Belgium, Scandinavia and other countries.   The representatives of Russia declared in substance that, in the
years that had elapsed since the former conventions
(1878 and 1881), they had seen no reasons for changing
their convictions against the feasibility of free-coinage
bimetallism, and cited examples showing how utterly
impossible it is in monetary matters to resist natural
forces by agreements or statutory laws.

In this connection it is well to recall the significant
remarks at the Brussels Convention of Mr. Tirard,
then Minister of Finance of the French Republic and
Governor of the Bank of France.   Said Mr. Tirard:

" *Despite all the demonstrations and the speeches, all
the publications and all the newspaper articles, do we see
the Powers named, and others too, change their opinion ?*
NOT THE LEAST IN THE WORLD."

And this applies at present with peculiar force to the expressions of some members of the Budapest Congress last August, encouraging the Populistic ideas of independent free coinage of silver by the United States. In short, will our people permit themselves to be made cat's paws of in experiments to determine whether such a course is safe for Europe when every such experiment in the history of civilization has been a failure?

To those who may be disposed to give ear to such delusive views, I recommend that they ponder the words of General Francis A. Walker, the ablest bimetallist of the United States, in the Boston *Herald* of September 9th, as follows:

"I think it is folly,—it is suicidal,—this attempt to identify the interests of bimetallism with the present free coinage agitation. I have conferred with leading bimetallists in Europe, and I find that they deprecate this movement in America. In all their advocacy of the remonetization of silver, they assume as a necessary condition that this free coinage shall not prevail."

I take the liberty, also, of applying here some remarks of the Hon. Thos. B. Reed:

"There must be addressed to us some solid arguments, or at least the opinions of wise men, who have proved their wisdom by the actual test of human life. Surely we are not going to venture into the unknown because these empiricists bid us do so while they still leave unproved every principle upon which they found their advice. So long as they cannot agree among themselves on any of their propositions, they cannot be cited as a body to force our conclusions. On no trackless future should we venture unless the prospect of increased happiness is large enough to justify risk and exposure. Is there any example in the history of the world of any nation situated like ours who has taken the step to which we are invited?"

As to the value of any agreement or understanding with Russia upon the subject, even if that government were disposed to make one, it would amount to nothing. She has more gold and silver now than she has bank notes in circulation, and as to the question of international trade or the world's commerce,—the main artery of the whole subject,—84 per cent of our transactions are with gold-standard countries, 7 per cent with depreciated paper countries, and only 9 per cent with silver-standard countries; hence any one can see at a glance the futility of promoting a monetary agreement with nations with which we scarcely transact any business. As a matter of fact Great Britain pays us more than $200,000,000 annually for products of this country, while Russia pays us but $4,000,000.

Mr. Newlands, on page twenty-two of his argument, speaks as follows:

"We have a certain duty, it seems to me, to the South American Republics, that now disgrace the name of republicanism, a certain duty to civilization and humanity, and we ought to discharge it, and one of the first steps is to put them on a sound money basis by gradually retiring their depreciated paper and substituting silver coin."

This is more altruistic than when in the first quotation above he desired to impair the efficiency of cheap labor, etc. However, it is in order for Mr. Newlands to consider the wise advice given us by the Father of Our

Country more than a hundred years ago in regard to entangling alliances. It is also in order for him to consider certain basic scientific truths, namely, that the purchasing power of money is not determined by kings, governments, congresses or conventions, but by the silent and unseen but invincible forces of universal self-interest. Nations, as nations, do not trade. To paraphrase Prof. Francis A. Walker, an international bimetallist: The normal working of the principle of self-interest is all we have to go by in dealing with matters of finance and currency. There is here no question of patriotism, philanthropy or sentiment. These last may have room to operate in the workshop, the warehouse, the factory, the railroad, the express office, the farm, but, in finance, none. All reasoning which assumes that in the exchange of moneys any principle can be substituted for that of individual self-interest must inevitably be futile and delusive. This is not cynicism, not avarice, not sordidness: it is the science of money, economic law, which we may accept as abiding. To deal with the subject on any other basis is not only erroneous, but will prove disastrous. If value and virtue could be created by legal enactment or conventional agreement, we would all have been wealthy and wise before now.

Another thing for Mr. Newlands to consider is why should the human race, at this particular stage of its development, be asked to deem a ratio of silver to gold of 16 to 1 as a divinely fixed and irrevocable relation when we know as a matter of fact that since the beginning of history the ratios commercially have varied from 1 of silver to 1 of gold to 34 of silver to 1 of gold.

What scientific reason can he advance for such a contention, while in a period of less than three thousand years the two metals have separated from an accepted value of ounce for ounce, and have moved along on diverging lines, until the relation has reached thirty odd ounces of one to one ounce of the other. In view of these facts, why should the United States declare to the wide world that the ratio shall, willy nilly, be 16 to 1? In short it would be a case of King Canute come to grief again.

The able Chairman of the Committee on Ways and Means, Hon. Nelson Dingley, of Maine, very tersely stated the gist of the matter, as it affects this country, when he asserted that the financial trouble in the United States arises from the fact that our government has paper out as currency, whereas no other gold-standard nation emits Government circulating notes. This is the radical defect of our monetary system.

I have asked why prices should not have fallen in the past twenty-five years. Prof. Shaler, in his "United States of America," says:

" The beginning of civilization has sometimes been fixed at the date, whenever it may have been, when man first set apart a lot of land, fenced it in or appropriated it, and then applied the force of a domesticated animal to his aid in the production of food. One can imagine how it was at the very beginning, when some one harnessed a bullock to a pointed stick, attached by a cord to the horns, beginning to plow. That primitive method of plowing still survives in some parts of the world. The fellahin of Egypt could be brought to an Exposition who still make use of the appliances of agriculture that are pictured upon the walls of the pyramids, and from the pointed stick, which may be taken as an example of the beginning of civilization itself, the whole progress in the development of the mechanism of agriculture could be brought before the eye in one building. The last example might be a great combined machine that has been applied by its inventor in the valleys of California to the production of wheat. By means of this mechanism the wheat field is plowed, harrowed, seeded, and rolled down in a single process. In the autumn the plows are detached, and a harvester worked by the same steam power is substituted,—thrashing, winnowing, and putting the wheat into bags in a single operation. The cost of the labor of man which is applied to the direction of this mechanism is less than one dollar an acre in each year; the whole cost of the labor, aside from the maintenance of the capital, is less than four cents on a bushel of wheat. The product for three hundred days' labor of one man, corresponding to a year's work, has been in some seasons over fifteen thousand bushels. The wheat is carried to the seaboard, loaded upon steamships, and moved to London to feed the hungry workman of Great Britain, whose customary loaf, called the quartern loaf, weighs four pounds. There is no coin in existence in Great Britain small enough to stand as a symbol of the labor cost or the proportionate part of the wages paid in California for producing wheat enough for that quartern loaf. There is but one coin in use in Great Britain, and that is seldom seen,—the farthing,—which would represent the cost of moving the wheat that is required in each quartern loaf from the field in California half way around the globe to the market in London."

Prof. Branner, in Sunday's *Chronicle*, mentions (what I have repeatedly referred to in former papers) that " every new discovery, every valuable invention, lowers prices and (*temporarily*) turns men out of work," and states that "in the year 1885 the use of natural gas in and about Pittsburg, Pa., replaced 3,650,000 tons of coal and displaced 5,000 men." Nevertheless the average prices of farm products generally, from 1873 to 1896, as shown by all the information obtainable on the subject, have been higher relatively than the average prices of transportation, manufactures, interest, etc. But suppose they had not: Shall the developments and applications of science be restricted or nullified by lowering our standard of value? Under the best standard of value—gold—wages in gold-using countries have risen in purchasing power seventy-five per cent during the past sixty years.

The disturbing effect on the practical condition of mankind, inseparable from the extraordinary spread and marvelous efficiency of mechanical contrivances and scientific appliances in the world's fields of industry, cannot be counteracted by a depreciated standard of value. No such phenomenon as the industrial advance of this generation has ever confronted mankind. M. Berthelot, in a paper recently read before European scientists, stated, substantially, that more has been done for the development of man during the last seventy-five years than in the preceding six thousand.

[*From News Letter, October 10, 1896.*]

Editor News Letter :

SIR : It seems almost absurd to present statistics to prove the remarkable progress of the human race during this century, yet the extraordinary assertions made by silver agitators have seemingly produced such a widespread feeling of unrest and discontent that it seems necessary to oppose fact to frenzy.

Senator Stewart said in the November, 1895, *Overland*:

"Does anybody doubt that Japan, China, Mexico, and other free-coinage countries, are more prosperous and happy than ever before in their history, *while every gold-standard country in the world is more miserable than at any other time for the last two hundred years ?*"

In an article on "Progress" in the *Overland* of the current month, I drew, for the past general condition of wage-earners in this country, from Prof. McMaster's "History of the People of the United States," and I will put him in evidence still further. He says, in his history, speaking of the proceedings of Congress on wages in 1794 :

"On the 6th of January a bill was reached, and a discussion provoked, which throws much light on the condition of laborers and mechanics. The matter under debate was the pay of the soldiers. Each private at that time received every four weeks, as compensation for the hunger and privations he suffered at the frontier posts, a sum not so great as is now paid to the most unskilled laborer for three days of toil. His hire was *three* dollars a month. Such wages a member thought were too small, and he would gladly see them raised to *five*. He could not, he said, hire a workman who was to sleep in peace in his bed, and eat his dinner in comfort at a table, for the pay that was given to a soldier for enduring the hardships and dangers of his calling. This was quickly denied. One told him that in the States north of Pennsylvania the wages which a common laborer took home with him each week were not superior to those of a soldier. Another declared that in Vermont good men were hired for eighteen pounds a year, which was equal to four dollars per month, and out of this found their clothes. The bill was thereupon laid upon the table."

From this period and during the continental war prices were variable, rising and falling in sympathy with the changes in affairs generally; but of wages in 1802 McMaster says:

"The condition of the wage-class of that day may well be examined; it is full of instruction for social agitators. In the great cities unskilled workmen were hired by the day, bought their own food, and found their own lodgings. But in the country, on the farms, or wherever a band was employed on some public work, they were fed and lodged by the employer and given a few dollars a month. On the Pennsylvania canals the diggers ate the coarsest diet, were housed in the rudest sheds, and paid six dollars a month from May to November, and five dollars a month from November to May. Hod-carriers and mortar-mixers, diggers and choppers, who, from 1795 to 1800, labored on the public buildings and cut the streets and avenues of Washington City, received seventy dollars a year, or, if they wished, sixty dollars for all the work they could perform from March 1st to December 20th. The hours of work were invariably from sunrise to sunset. Wages at Albany and New York were three shillings, or, as money then went, forty cents a day; at Lancaster, eight or ten dollars a month; elsewhere in Pennsylvania workmen were content with six dollars in summer and five in winter. At Baltimore men were glad to be hired at eighteen pence a day. None, by the month, asked more than six dollars. At Fredericksburg the price of labor was from five to seven dollars. In Virginia white men employed by the year were given sixteen pounds currency; slaves, when hired, were clothed, and their masters paid one pound a month. A pound

Virginia money was, in Federal money, three dollars
and thirty-three cents. The average rate of wages the
land over was, therefore, sixty-five dollars a year, with
food and, perhaps, lodging. Out of this small sum the
workman must, with his wife's help, maintain his
family. Typesetters were paid twenty-five cents a
thousand ems, and even this rate, the publishers com-
plained, made as much as eight dollars a week. Such
great wages, combined with the cost of type, paper and
clerks, induced the publishers of six newspapers in the
city of New York to combine and put up the price of
subscription from eight to ten dollars a year."

Prof. Nathaniel S. Shaler, in his "United States of
America," tabulates the progress in money, wages or
earnings as follows:

	1850. Gold.	1891. Gold.
Foremen, overseers, master mechanics, head car-penters, boss machinists, etc.	$2.00	$4.25
Carpenters, masons, machinists, printers, etc.	1.47	2.60
Operatives in factories and workshops of many kinds	.90	1.49
Laborers in factories, workshops, gas works, brickyards, and other occupations in continuous employment	.90	1.46
Passenger-car conductors on extensive lines of railway	2.11	3.84
	1840.	1890.
Firemen in extensive gas works	1.20	3.00

Workmen in New York gas works, firemen's wages, 1845 to
1850 inclusive, were $1.20 per day; 1885 to 1890, $3.00; increase,
150 per cent.

"The above examples are selected from among many
of like kind, all of which were governed by the
same rule which establishes the rate of wages. The
same rule holds in every branch of industry subject to
occasional variations due to special causes. The evidence is, however, conclusive, that while all rates of
wages have nearly or quite doubled in the last fifty
years the hours of labor have been much reduced, yet

the purchasing power of each dollar is now substantially the same as it was in 1850. The advance in wages has been in proportion to the relative skill required. The skilled laborers have gained the most, the common laborers the least."

But, it may be asked, how about the present? To meet such a query I append the following, somewhat abridged, from Mr. L. N. Dembitz's monograph on "The Free Silver Problem," which demonstrates that wages are now on an average higher in gold than they were in 1873 in gold:

	1873 Paper.	1873 Gold.	1895. Gold.
Street repairs:			
Bricklayers	$4.50	$3.89½	$5.00
Stonecutters	3.25	2.81	3.75
Laborers	1.62½	1.41	1.50
Teams	4.00	3.46	3.50
Street cleaning:			
Foremen	2.50	2.16¼	2.00
Laborers	1.50	1.29¾	1.37½
Teams	4.00	3.46	3.25
Railroad locomotive engineers	3.50	3.02¾	4.32½
Railroad locomotive firemen	2.03¾	1.69	2.80
Machinists	2.57½	2.23	2.91½
Carpenters	3.21	2.85½	2.04½
Painters	2.43¾	2.24	2.25
Track laborers	1.64	1.42	1.08
Other laborers	1.71¼	1.58	1.36¼
Telegraphers, per month	110.00	95.15	85.00
Laborers on earthworks, per day	1.25	1.08	1.25
Printers, per day	3.50	3.02¾	3.00
Printers, per thousand ems	.45	.39	.40
Bookbinders, per week	20.33⅓	17.60	16.50
Molders, per day	3.00	2.69½	2.25
Carpenters, per day	3.16⅔	2.73⅔	2.16⅔
Plasterers, per day	4.00	3.46	4.50
Tanners (by day in 1873, now by piece, but with less hours of work), per week	11.00	9.25	14.50
Laborers in tanneries, per week	7.50	6.48½	7.50
Female teachers, per month:			
High schools	80.00	69.20	90.00
Intermediate schools	60.00	51.90	63.00
District schools	50.00	43.25	52.00

Now let us compare for 1864, paper currency, the prices of certain fabrics and other manufactured articles, with 1894, gold currency.

	1864.	1894.
American prints, per yard	$ .20	$ .05½
Ginghams, per yard	.20	.06⅞
Canton flannel, per yard.................	.30	.09
Denim, per yard........................	.20	.12½
Pepperell corset jeans, per yard	.25	.08
Sheeting, per yard......................	.29	.08
Sugar, refined, per pound...............	.22	.04½
Carpets, ingrain, two-ply	1.63	.51
Nails, per 100-pound keg...............	7.85	1.08
Window glass, per 50 feet, 10 x 12	5.08	1.99
Steel rails, per ton, 1867...............	166.00	24.00
Freight rates, per ton mile	.03$\frac{8}{10}$	.00$\frac{76}{100}$

And manufactures, as a rule, have fallen in price relatively.

One hundred and fifty years ago the average rate for skilled and unskilled labor in Great Britain and Continental Europe was less than twenty-five cents per day ; now it is four times that. A speech of the Hon. Thos. B. Reed is my authority for the statement that in 1725 the wages of mechanics, such as carpenters, bricklayers, etc., were but twenty-five cents per day in England. Thos. Jefferson in his correspondence, while resident in Paris, speaks of the pay of French country women laborers being eight cents per day.

For the condition of the masses in England I will put in evidence Walter Besant, in "Fifty Years Ago." He says that one hundred and fifty years ago there was no religion, no morality, no education, no knowledge. The people were devoured by epidemic diseases or prematurely killed by liquor. No virtue at all seemed to exist except bull-dog pluck and tenacity. There are glimpses which show conditions of existence so shockingly wretched that any cheerfulness whatever was amazing. In England "Father Stick" kept all in subjection. The first law to protect children in the factories was passed in 1802, limiting time to twelve hours daily for women and children; but this was at first evaded, and thirteen to fourteen hours were exacted, which, the chronicler says, was of itself a little heaven to what had previously existed. In 1833 a law was passed restricting child labor to those over nine years of age, and that children under thirteen should not work more than forty-eight hours a week, and those under eighteen not more than sixty-eight hours a week. Next came reform of labor in the mine pits, where children six years of age were then worked twelve hours a day.

It may be claimed that these statements are exaggerated, but they are furnished by an eminent living author in the city of London, and he says of sixty years ago: The authorities stripped women to the waist and lashed them at Bridewell; they caught the apprentices and flogged them soundly; lashed the criminal at the cart tail, lashed the prisoners, lashed soldiers in the army, and sailors on board ships, lashed the boys in school; in short, everybody was kept in order or subjection by "Father Stick;" and under his rule there was no education, no religion, no morals. The masses were left entirely to themselves to go from bad to worse; more thirsty of gin, more brutal, more ignorant; so that in the long run there was not under the light of the sun a more depraved and degraded race than that which peopled the lowest levels of the great towns of England.

Besant says substantially: In the fifteen years from 1825 to 1840, 50,000 convicts were sent to the penal settlements of Australasia, and the law recognized two hundred and twenty-seven capital offenses; nor was it until in the sixties that all the atrocious penal laws were finally swept from the statute books. The conditions of the average social life in the way of profligacy, licentiousness, drunkenness and pugilism, unrestrained fighting of both sexes, was something almost impossible to conceive of at the present time. It was not safe to expose articles of value in the shop windows.

The relief of the poor in England in 1834, with 16,000,000 of population, cost $35,000,000; in 1844 conditions had so improved that it only cost $25,000,000, and the present time shows a still greater improvement.

Sixty years ago 40 per cent of the men and 65 per cent of the women could neither read nor write; all the grammar schools were controlled by the Church of England, and the children of non-conformists were not permitted to attend. As for the education of women, there was none in the classical sense. In 1837 there were 4,000 people subsisting in London by literary work, while at present there are over 16,000.

In 1836 an English writer, referring to the construction of railroads, predicted that the mail would ultimately be carried by rail from London to Liverpool in 10 hours; the time is now 3 hours and 50 minutes.

The first great victory of the long struggle for better things was the Reform Act of 1832, which began to teach the people the art of self-government. Then began and moved on with increasing rapidity the spread of the non-conformist sects, and the multiplication of chapels and religious services throughout the land. It is added that previous to this time nine out of ten of the working people were avowed infidels, and that not one man in a hundred ever even opened a Bible.

There can be no doubt of the remarkable improvement in the general condition of the people; though the rich have become richer the poor have not become poorer. The skilled worker is better paid now than then; his work is more steady; his working hours are lessened; he is better clothed, better educated, better mannered; has more leisure for recreation, for social life; can combine in his business, co-operate with his fellow-workman, hold meetings and vote; has better and cheaper newspapers; better food and at less cost; is vastly better housed, and accumulates means rapidly, as the deposits in savings banks attest. Not only is he actually better off, but, considered with the richer classes, he is relatively better off. His amusements have no longer the same brutality as formerly.

Robert Giffen says, in his " Progress of the Working Classes in the Last Half Century: "

" What we have to consider is, that sixty years ago the workingman with wages, on the average about half, or not much more than half, what they are now, had at times to contend with a fluctuation in the price of bread, which implied sheer starvation. Periodic starvation was, in fact, the condition of the masses of workingmen throughout the kingdom sixty years ago, and the references to the subject in the economic literature of the time are most instructive.

" Fresh meat sixty years ago was not an article of the workingman's diet, as it has since become. He had little more concern with its price than with the price of diamonds.

" The working classes have had large additions to their means; capital has increased in about equal ratio, but the increase of capital per head of the capitalist classes is by no means so great as the increase of working-class incomes.

"The war of the land nationalizer and Populist is then not so much with the capitalist as with the workman, and the importance of this fact should not be lost sight of."

French statisticians have asserted that in the eighteenth century the peasants in many parts of France paid away four-fifths of their incomes to the State Treasurer. They did not earn, on an average, a franc (20 cents) per day. Taine says:

"The garret and the hut as well as the farm and the farmhouse knew the tax-gatherer, the constable and the bailiff. No hovel escaped the detestable brood. The people sow, harvest, work and undergo privations for their benefit ; and, should the farthings so painfully saved each week amount at the end of the year to a piece of silver, the mouth of the official pouch closed over it."

Another writer asks what these peasants were, and answers :

"They were savage-looking beings, black, livid and sunburnt, digging and grubbing at the soil from sunrise to sunset with invincible stubbornness, and retiring at night into their *dens*, where they lived on black bread, water and roots."

Saint Simon says of 1725 :

"The people in Normandy lived on the grass of the fields. In the most prosperous days of Fleury, and in the finest region in France, the peasant hides his wine on account of the excise, and his bread on account of the taille, convinced that he is a lost man (*pecuniarily*) if any doubt exists of his dying of starvation."

D'Argenson writes of 1739:

"In the canton of Touraine men have been eating herbage more than a year, while in the bishopric of Chartres the famine and the mortality were such that men ate grass like sheep and died like flies."

Taine says that the country was abandoned by the spade and the plow, and a vast portion of the soil ceased to feed men, while the rest, poorly cultivated, scarcely provided the smallest necessities.

Massillon wrote to Fleury in 1740:

"The people of the rural districts are living in frightful destitution, without beds, without furniture. The majority for half a year even lack barley and oat bread, *their sole food*, and which they are compelled to take out of their own and their children's mouths to pay taxes."

Massillon says of the same year at Chattellerault:

"The poor outnumber those able to live without begging, while prosecutions for unpaid dues are carried on with unexampled rigor; and the clothes of the poor are seized, and their last measure of flour, even the latches on their doors, are taken by the tax gatherer."

D'Argenson writes of ten years later:

"In the country around me, ten leagues from Paris, I find increased privation. What must it be in our wretched provinces in the interior, where the collectors, with their officers, accompanied by locksmiths, force open the doors and carry off and sell furniture for one-quarter of its value. I see the people dying of destitution. Some of the seigniors of Touraine inform me that, being desirous of setting the inhabitants to work by the day, they found very few of them, and those so weak from privation that they were unable to use their arms."

Taine says of 1753 that at Paris one finds in the Fauburg St. Antoine over 800 persons dying of privation in a single month; that the poor expire with cold and hunger in their garrets, without any possible relief.

Of 1760 another observer says that one-fourth of the soil of France was lying waste, and in Auvergne the country is being depopulated. In 1784 the assembly of Haute Garonne said that the lot of the most severely taxed communities is so rigorous as to have led their proprietors frequently to abandon their property. In Gascony the spectacle is heartrending.

I could extend these examples indefinitely, but space will not permit. The conditions in Germany and elsewhere in Europe were not better.

Walter Besant, to resume his pertinent comments, further says of England:

"It is commonplace to talk of the leisure and calm of the eighteenth century: it cannot be too often repeated that in 1837 we were still in that century. I declare that in all my reading about social life in the eighteenth century I have failed to discover that leisure. From Queen Anne to Victoria I have searched for it, and I cannot find it. The leisure of the eighteenth century exists only in the brain of the painter and poet. Life was hard; labor was incessant, and lasted the whole day long; the shopmen lived in the shop— they slept in it; the mill people worked all day long and far into the night. If I look about the country I see in town and village the poor man oppressed and driven by his employer; I see the laborer in a blind revenge setting fire to the ricks; I see the factory-hand destroying the machinery; I see everywhere discontent, poverty, privilege, patronage and profligacy; I hear the shrieks of the wretches flogged at Bridewell; I see the white faces of the poor creatures brought out to be hung up in rows for stealing bread; I see the fighting of the press-gang; I see the soldiers and sailors flogged into sullen obedience; I see hatred of the Church, hatred of the governing classes, hatred of the rich, hatred of employers: Where, with all these things, was there room for leisure?"

The foregoing comparisons strikingly exhibit some of the beneficent changes of this century. What are the losses? Is there as much of reverence as fifty years ago? Is there manly, courageous independence in partisan politics? Is the generally superficial education of the day an unmixed blessing? Is the license of the press a boon? Cowper tell us that

"Knowledge, when wisdom is too weak to guide her,
Is like a headstrong horse that throws the rider."

However, despite any and all misgivings, I think we may agree that the world moves. We have present evidence of manly independence in national politics. However defective education is it is better than in the past. A sensational press is better than no press or a gagged press; and gentler manners, purer laws, prevail. The aggregate of rationality, moderation, temperance and virtue is ever increasing, and yet the ideal humanity is afar off, and we cannot too strongly emphasize Lowell's expression:

"The measure of a nation's true success is the amount it has contributed to the thought, the moral energy, the intellectual happiness, the spiritual hope and consolation of mankind."

JOHN J. VALENTINE.

[*P. S. to News Letter article of October 10th.*]

In my communication of September 5th, I mentioned that the present wealth of California is some $2,100 per capita, the greatest of any State in the Union. This was assumed from the fact that it is about double the average for the whole United States; but, in looking at the Census of 1890, I find that several of the Pacific Coast or Rocky Mountain States exceed this sum per capita; and in view of the wild crusade in behalf of cheap money as a panacea for the asserted deplorable effects of the alleged demonetization of silver in the United States, it is well to compare property valuations for the Rocky Mountain or Pacific Coast group of States, eleven in number, as reported .in the Census of 1870 and in that of 1890. They are as follows, and carry their own lesson :

The Valuation of Real and Personal Property.

	TOTAL.		PER CAPITA.	
	1870.	1890.	1870.	1890.
Montana	$ 15,184,522	$ 453,135,209	$ 737	$3,429
Wyoming	7,016,748	169,773,710	770	2,797
Colorado	20,243,303	1,145,712,267	508	2,780
New Mexico...	31,349,793	231,459,897	341	1,507
Arizona	3,440,791	188,880,976	356	3,168
Utah	16,159,995	349,411,234	186	1,681
Nevada	31,134,012	180,323,668	733	3,941
Idaho.........	6,552,681	207,896,591	437	2,464
Washington ...	13,562,164	760,698,726	566	2,177
Oregon........	51,558,932	590,396,194	567	1,882
California.....	638,768,017	2,533,733,627	1,140	2,097
	$834,969,958	$6,811,422,099	$ 843	$2,250

The increase throughout the whole United States from 1870 to 1890 was 116 per cent, or from 28,000 million dollars (Mulhall), or 30,000 million dollars (U. S. Census), to 65,000 million dollars, according to the latter. In the extreme Western group, as shown above, it was simply amazing—from 834 million dollars in 1870 to 6,811 million dollars in 1890; or over 700 per cent. Colorado, for example, increased from 20 million dollars to 1,145 million dollars. Where does the depreciation of values by reason of the "*Crime against silver*" come in? That there was inflation in these vast expansions of value cannot be doubted. That contraction has ensued was inevitable, and therefore is not to be wondered at.

JOHN J. VALENTINE.